theatre & politics

Theatre&
Series Standing Order: ISBN 978–0–230–20327–3 paperback

You can receive further titles in this series as they are published by placing a standing order. Please contact your bookseller or, in the case of difficulty, write to us at the address below with your name and address, the title of the series, and the ISBN quoted above.

Customer Services Department, Palgrave Macmillan Ltd.
Houndmills, Basingstoke, Hampshire, RG21 6XS, England

theatre & politics

Joe Kelleher

palgrave
macmillan

First published 2009 by
PALGRAVE MACMILLAN

Palgrave Macmillan in the UK is an imprint of Macmillan Publishers Limited, registered in England, company number 785998, of Houndmills, Basingstoke, Hampshire RG21 6XS.

Palgrave Macmillan in the US is a division of St Martin's Press LLC, 175 Fifth Avenue, New York, NY 10010.

Palgrave Macmillan is the global academic imprint of the above companies and has companies and representatives throughout the world.

Palgrave® and Macmillan® are registered trademarks in the United States, the United Kingdom, Europe and other countries.

ISBN-13: 978–0–230–20523–9 paperback
ISBN-10: 0–230–20523–2 paperback

This book is printed on paper suitable for recycling and made from fully managed and sustained forest sources. Logging, pulping and manufacturing processes are expected to conform to the environmental regulations of the country of origin.

A catalogue record for this book is available from the British Library.

A catalog record for this book is available from the Library of Congress.

10 9 8 7 6 5 4 3 2 1
18 17 16 15 14 13 12 11 10 09

Printed and bound in China

contents

series editors' preface

The theatre is everywhere, from entertainment districts to the fringes, from the rituals of government to the ceremony of the courtroom, from the spectacle of the sporting arena to the theatres of war. Across these many forms stretches a theatrical continuum through which cultures both assert and question themselves.

Theatre has been around for thousands of years, and the ways we study it have changed decisively. It's no longer enough to limit our attention to the canon of Western dramatic literature. Theatre has taken its place within a broad spectrum of performance, connecting it with the wider forces of ritual and revolt that thread through so many spheres of human culture. In turn, this has helped make connections across disciplines; over the past fifty years, theatre and performance have been deployed as key metaphors and practices with which to rethink gender, economics, war, language, the fine arts, culture and one's sense of self.

Theatre & is a long series of short books which hopes to capture the restless interdisciplinary energy of theatre and performance. Each book explores connections between theatre and some aspect of the wider world, asking how the theatre might illuminate the world and how the world might illuminate the theatre. Each book is written by a leading theatre scholar and represents the cutting edge of critical thinking in the discipline.

We have been mindful, however, that the philosophical and theoretical complexity of much contemporary academic writing can act as a barrier to a wider readership. A key aim for these books is that they should all be readable in one sitting by anyone with a curiosity about the subject. The books are challenging, pugnacious, visionary sometimes and, above all, clear. We hope you enjoy them.

Jen Harvie and Dan Rebellato

theatre & politics

Politics

I'm looking at a photograph taken by Luiz Vasconcelos that was printed in my daily newspaper this morning ('Eyewitness 11.03.08', *Guardian*, 13 March 2008). It is a picture of something that was happening this week on the other side of the world from south London, where I am writing this book. The photograph was taken in a place called Manaus in Brazil. It's a striking image which shows a line of riot police marching towards us, their black steel-and-wood shields forming an unbroken wall in front of their bodies, so you don't see their faces, just their armoured kneepads and grey combat trousers and black shiny boots stomping over the dry, brown earth. In front of the advancing police line, her back up against one of the shields, her hand holding onto another, her eyes shut tight, her mouth open to shout or scream, is a woman in a T-shirt and coloured skirt holding against her side an infant who is naked except for a pair of blue plastic sandals. A wooden truncheon (we see no hand attached to it) comes out from behind a shield in the centre of the picture, suspended above the woman's head, about to strike or just after impact. The woman is wearing the same sort of sandals as her child. Her feet are braced against the earth.

A caption informs us that the image is of an incident at a dispute near the Amazonian rainforest in northwest Brazil, where police expelled members of the Landless Workers Movement (Movimento dos Trabalhadores Rurais Sem Terra) from a privately owned tract of land. 'In Brazil,' we are told, 'where 1.6% of landlords control 46% of the arable land, the Landless Workers Movement encourages people to occupy and farm unused land.' According to the movement's website, it is 'the largest social movement in Latin America with an estimated 1.5 million landless members organized in 23 out [of] 27 states' (www.mstbrazil.org). Whatever we understand politics to be about, it is likely to have something to do with what is brought to our attention in this picture.

Before looking more closely at the picture, however, we should ask ourselves what we mean by this term 'politics'. Any search for a definition of politics is going to turn up a range of different understandings, depending for instance on whether the term is taken to refer to the activities of government and other social systems and organisations, or to the *study* of such activities and systems, or to the processes by which power is distributed – and struggled over – in society more generally. As a starting-point for the present discussion, I offer the following formulation by the writer Stefan Collini. In an article titled 'On Variousness; and on Persuasion' (2004), Collini defines politics as 'the important, inescapable, and difficult attempt to determine relations of power in a given space' (p. 67). By the phrase 'relations of power' we might understand that power – or powerlessness – is nothing in itself and only ever meaningful in terms of the distribution of power across social relations, among different groups or classes or interests that make up, however momentarily, a social body. It goes without saying that this distribution of power is often unequal.

Collini's definition is valuable not only for his focus on questions of power and relations but also for the implication that shaping and determining these questions is not straightforward and is likely to be contested, and that the process of politics is ongoing – indeed, as far as we can see, endless. Although he is not writing about theatre, Collini's focus on 'a given space' is also helpful to us in the context of our discussion of theatre and politics, as so much of what we consider in the pages to come involves our continually pulling focus between one space and another – for example, between the 'given' space of the theatrical stage and the imagined space of the outside world, which the stage-play world of the theatre relates to in so many complex ways. It is also probably worth emphasising at the start that this book is intended as an exploration of theatre *and politics* rather than of 'political theatre'. I do discuss political theatre in a later section, exploring some twentieth-century theatrical attempts to engage in social relations in ways that would have a direct political effect on the world outside the theatre. That discussion is only part, though, of a wider engagement in the following pages with how theatricality can be thought of *in relation to* politics, neither focusing exclusively on theatre that has been designated 'political' nor assuming that all theatre is political in some general way (although it may well be that any piece of theatre can be discussed in terms of its specific political dimensions).

We shall come back to these matters soon. Leaving theatre aside for a moment and returning to our photograph, we could say that the politics involved in this image touches on two related, but in some ways distinct, scenes. One is the scene of bodies and forces that the published photograph makes visible, in which violence and vulnerability, power and exclusion, are matters for those particular people in that particular place; in that moment, politics is a matter of what hurts and what breaks right now, of the immediate struggle of interests and passions in a situation of danger and panic and on-the-spot actions. The other scene involves the larger, public space of the Landless Workers Movement and the contexts in which its struggles take place. These contexts involve mass membership, particular modes of administration and debate and education, literacy programmes, and legal dispute at both a local and a state level over provisions in the Brazilian constitution for the 'social use' of unfarmed land. This larger scene, in which politics is a matter of slow, hard work, of patience and organisation, of histories located deep in the past and hopes extended far into the future, is not necessarily separable from that first scene, but it is less easily represented in a picture or photograph.

In both scenes – the one in which a woman is struck by a police truncheon while her child clings to her side and the one of mass movements and local organisation, of legal disputes over constitutional clauses and the right to work the land – 'politics' has to do with the same basic concerns. These are concerns about participation, ownership, membership, and exclusion. They involve questions of who – or what – does or does not 'count' as a member or owner or worker or citizen. These are questions too of how that count might be contested (the actions that people will take, the things they actually *do* to change the situation) and also how that contestation is opposed by those in power (in this instance, by deploying the police). Furthermore, as we become aware of the still wider geopolitical context in which these events take place – of issues of international debt and competition over resources, the global movement of capital, goods, and people, and the ways that wealth in one part of the world may be dependent upon poverty in another – 'we' may be less than certain that these are questions about scenes being played out far away from us. These concerns are also, in all sorts of ways, likely to be 'our' concerns, whoever we may be, and wherever we may happen to find ourselves as we encounter the scene.

There is also, though, a politics to do with our encounter with the scene as such. The fact that we encounter the scene as a photograph itself raises complications, given that this photograph, like any other, is at once detached from the reality it represents (I am looking at a picture of Manaus from five thousand miles away in London) and at the same time dependent on that absent reality for its significance, and so in a sense still attached to a past moment in a faraway place. Any determination of the relations of power in *this* given space is going to have to take a certain amount on trust. Such complications are exacerbated, of course, by the fact that you are not even looking at the photograph but reading my description of the image. To which description I add the following: we can observe that whatever the image does show, there is also a great deal that it cannot show. Even if we allow that there are all sorts of ways in which an image *can* include what is going on outside its frame (for example, through the focus and attention of figures within the image on something out of shot) and can also make reference to what happened before and after the event it records (any sort of clue will do, such as a footprint, a shadow, a bruise, a facial expression), even so the image is partial, in the sense that it shows only part of the story it is telling. The image is also partial in another sense of the word, to do with attachment and bias of judgement: partial, for instance, in the sort of political sympathies it appears to express, on the part of the makers and publishers and likely readers of the image, about the events it depicts. In this respect we could point to the way the image is captioned (could another caption imply a different political viewpoint?) and to the prominence it is given as a double-page colour spread in the middle of a liberal broadsheet newspaper like the *Guardian*, either of which can colour the politics both of the image itself and of our responses.

There are also, though, 'facts' of the image, not the least of which is the fact that the only human-looking beings in the photograph are that woman and her naked child, backed up against the 'faceless' wall of advancing riot police. As fellow humans, presumably we know which side we are supposed to be on, although even that depends upon our assumptions as to what humanity is supposed to look like and our readiness to let any particular example stand in for the species as a whole. That readiness has not always been forthcoming, as we discuss later. There are further complications. In the image the woman is isolated, but a closer look at the photograph reveals that in the hand that is clasped around her child she is holding what looks like a mobile phone. I also notice that at the edge of the image the face of one of the policemen can just be seen peering over his shield. These details begin to complicate the drama of isolation and connectedness that the image stages and the basic oppositions between exposed, fleshly, vulnerable humanity and a seemingly dehumanised, state-sponsored, mechanised violence, around which the politics of the image appears to be structured. Even so, there is a basic situation represented in this image, which we can call a political situation and which involves the paradoxical exclusion of an indigenous woman from the land that she needs to work on to feed herself and her child. As such, it is an image of a type that we became familiar with during the twentieth century, of humans exposed as vulnerable life-forms to the violence of large-scale, technologised, political machines: in the extreme case of the political systems that produced the Holocaust and the Gulags, these were systems of government and social organisation as geared up to the destruction of actual humans as they were to the production of forms of human community.

Given that the image draws our attention to what I have been referring to as a political 'scene', our question now, for an investigation that aims to open a consideration of politics and *theatre*, is the following: what happens to the politics when it is encountered like this, by us and others, as a sort of dramaturgy? That is to say, not as that woman encounters it, with her back to the advancing shields, her arm around her child, her eyes tight shut, and her mouth open to shout something that we cannot hear. Nor as it is encountered by the photographer Luiz Vasconcelos, who has a particularly privileged relationship to the event as he negotiates accident and chance and contingency for what can be captured and provisionally fixed and sent around the world. But encountered as we encounter it, as the ones who see the image or hear someone else describe it. This is not unlike the ways we encounter things in the theatre (or the ways we come across accounts of the theatre sometimes in theatre studies writing), where the scene does not just happen of its own accord but is put together in a particular way for our benefit, which means also put together to 'work' on us in particular ways.

In such instances we may respond to what works on us, with sympathy perhaps or indignation: sympathy for those whose roles in the drama appear to be already written, already distributed; indignation at events that take place before our eyes without our being able to intervene or do anything about them. And maybe all we can do sometimes, as readers, as spectators of the scene, is roll with the bias and register our own partiality, even while that woman still stands there, moments before the truncheon falls – as surely it will fall – and those shiny boots march onwards, although never quite marching out of the scene to where they can do any harm to *us*. We may feel, intuitively, this sense of detachment from what is going on, even as we take in and reflect upon the 'politics' of it all, if we imagine ourselves turning aside from the actual events in Manaus to a theatrical representation of those events. This representation might be a staged reconstruction of the newspaper photograph; or else a drama of scenes and speeches and gestures that seeks to illustrate, or explain, or argue with, or affect the situation in Manaus; or even a 'forum' of the sort established by the Brazilian theatre-maker and activist Augusto Boal, whom I discuss later in this book: an event that would include the woman herself, her child, and maybe also the policeman whose face we glimpse behind his shield, along with others whose interests are involved here, debating their concerns, staging their respective relations to the situation. We might feel that the theatrical event, however engaged or engaging, however sharp its analysis, however 'authentic' its elements, and however 'real' its representations, can only ever be less real and less significant than the event itself and the situation of inequality and conflict out of which it arises. At least for someone whose child is, literally, in the firing line and who is herself about to be cracked on the head by a truncheon.

At the same time, and no less intuitively (and I am assuming here that our intuitions are where we locate the sort of knowledge that has been hard thought for and that we find worth trusting), we may feel there is much in the way theatre goes about its business that still appears to lend itself to 'the important, inescapable, and difficult attempt' to engage with politics, in the theatre's given space as well as in any other. This political-ready quality of theatre includes its liveness and sociality, the simple fact that it happens *now* and that it gathers people, who may well be strangers to each other, around issues of disagreement but also of common concern. There is further political potential in the theatre's capacity to pretend, to say and show things that are not so and hence to propose alternative realities to how things are at present. There is potential too in the ways that theatre, among many other art forms, speaks 'for' us and 'of' our worlds, not to mention the worlds of others. The theatre 'represents' us, both in the sense of showing us images of ourselves and in the sense of standing in and standing up for us, like a delegate or a substitute or – indeed – a political representative. Theatre represents our lives to us in ways that can persuade us to make judgements on the quality and fidelity of those representations and to make critical judgements too on the lives that are so represented. This second intuition – to do with the 'efficacy' of an art form such as theatre, its power to produce effects – can impress itself upon us with such force we may feel that our theatre *should* have no other business than responding to situations like the one in Manaus. Furthermore, we may at least *hope* that if the response is tuned right – as regards, say, the commitment that goes into the work, the realism of the representation, and the canniness of the staging and the associations it establishes with people, places, times, and ideas – then the theatre can even make a difference to what is going on in Manaus, or if not in Manaus somewhere like it.

These are the sorts of hopes and intuitions we find in that dream of a 'political theatre' that haunted so much twentieth-century theatrical experiment. This is a dream that continues to inform the anxieties and uncertainties of our own times, when the business of resistant politics, given the all-consuming globalisation of political and cultural economies, can seem more intractable than ever. Even as we wake from that dream we may continue to ask ourselves: what am I doing, either as maker or spectator, when I 'do' theatre, especially when the theatre I do resembles the politics I only imagine?

We are back with the questions raised above when we considered the politics of the Manaus photograph, questions that drive the rest of our discussion and that now take the following basic form: what happens to the politics when it takes on scenic, dramaturgical form and circulates through the sort of spectacular economies and across the sort of distances that theatre deals in? A range of considered answers have been given to that question, several of which I consider in this book. One answer is summed up in the proposal of literary critic Fredric Jameson in *Brecht and Method* (2000) that theatre *is* 'political, not only in its formal effects, but also [in] that it is itself a figure for the social more generally, which it seeks to divide and set against itself' (p. 72). Jameson is referring to a range of complex effects, in Bertolt

Brecht's work particularly, to do with the way the action of a play *represents* various forms of social organisation and conflict, in the dual senses of 'representation' I suggested earlier. The play also then stirs up conflict in the immediate social body – the audience – that is there in the theatre to partake of this representation. Another sort of response, as argued more recently by theatre theorist Alan Read in *Theatre, Intimacy & Engagement* (2007), would be that the 'political' – as a mode of representation that tends towards 'fixing' the relations between things, as in a picture – is actually what gets in the way of politics. In Read's account, which is not so much a disagreement with the sort of argument put forward by Jameson as a continuation of a concern shared by many thinkers and practitioners for a politics 'of' performance, politics is figured as a continuing process that eludes representation, to the extent that any productive thinking of theatre and politics would do well to separate the two so that each can do its work more effectively, to the benefit of both (pp. 25–6).

All this is to say that, at the very least, the arguments are complex, as are the entanglements of nationality and statehood, class and ethnicity, land reform and constitutional law, global economics and local postcolonial struggle, Marxism and liberation theology involved in the politics of the Landless Workers Movement. Even so, we may want to invoke our intuitions one last time at this stage of the discussion and remark that there is also something overwhelmingly simple (and not, for that reason, necessarily untrue or insignificant) in the image of this woman and her child backed up against the police shields. It is the sort of 'truth', indeed, to which the arts of presentation and representation such as theatre and photography will always have a special access. As I have been arguing throughout this first section, from Collini's emphasis on politics as a difficult and in many ways intractable process of working out relations of power in a given situation, through a discussion of the politics involved in presenting and encountering political struggles in a composed, framed, and circulated image or in a dramatised scene, there are all sorts of ways in which we might want – or feel compelled – to *take care* of such truths. To a large extent this has to do with our recognising that the scenes that appear only to play before us in an external world 'out there' also involve ourselves; that we are also in the picture, that we may also be actors in the scene, even when the picture is of events taking place on the other side of the globe. One way of thinking about this would be to remember some of our richest theatre experiences: the ways in which any of the theatre that you – or I – have seen has engaged us personally and the ways in which this engagement had to do with feeling ourselves somehow involved in things going on in other times and other places. Another, seemingly different but actually related approach to taking care in the theatre is suggested by theatre historian Tracy C. Davis in her 2004 essay on 'Theatricality and Civil Society'. There she argues that as would-be politically engaged spectators of the public scene we should take a lesson from the twentieth-century political theatre and teach ourselves, when events such as those in Manaus are going on in front of our eyes, not to sympathise but to 'think'. Davis proposes standing 'aside from the suffering of the righteous to ... thus bring into being the self-possession of a critical stance' (p. 154). For Davis this critical stance enables us to identify unnatural acts (actions of cruelty and injustice, for instance, that we refuse to accept as necessary or inevitable aspects of life) where otherwise we might have taken for granted naturalised images (images that we accept without thinking as statements of truth about 'how things are'). In grasping hold of the act that produces an image we put ourselves in a position to do something about what we see, to conceive new laws for instance; in short, to do politics.

Davis's concern in her essay is more with the theatricality and social dramaturgy of public life and civil society than with actual theatre as such. Whether *theatre* can still provoke or enable us to do politics in this way is a question we have yet to consider. In much of what follows, I suggest that it may be in theatre's unreliability, its seeming fragility and tendency to *un*truth, its tendency to cast a mask over its own face, and its inability – politically speaking – to stop the police when they march forward, that its greatest political potential is to be found. I pursue these ideas in the next section with a close reading of a particular piece of theatre. We shall see how questions of violence and victimhood and the politics of 'representation' set out in a play are complicated by the unsettling effects of an actor's live performance and the unpredictable (and in some ways unknowable) responses of actual audiences. Later sections dig deeper into and wider across theatre history, focusing by and large on the work of actors on the theatrical stage and on the sorts of pleasure to be derived from watching the actors do their work. I explore, for example, ways in which theatre has both exploited and undermined the unreliable 'powers of persuasion' that are used to mark out the false and the true, the weak and the strong – in society and also on the theatrical stage. I look then at arguments, first set out by the ancient Greek philosophers, that deal with our enjoyment of the persuasive powers of theatrical imitations and also of the collapse and hollowing out of that power. As I argue in the section on 'Political Theatre', we could do worse, if our concern is with the relations between theatre and politics, than to think of the theatre as primarily a place of entertainment, a place where work and enjoyment are dependent one on the other and where politics has to do with the qualities, tensions, and implications of that dependence. However, we may also want to re-think what we usually mean by the word 'entertainment', allowing ourselves, for example, to 'entertain' the thought of theatre as a sort of signalling machine, prone sometimes to breakdown and irrelevance and miscommunication, not necessarily *doing* politics in any obvious way but bringing to the attention of us, its participants – actors and spectators all – the fact that some 'thing', some familiar stranger, is making an appearance here tonight and has a claim to make upon us. Our work, as this book attempts to argue, involves figuring out how we might respond to the justice of that claim.

For the moment, and to end this first section, we would do well to remind ourselves briefly of a key aspect of Collini's definition of politics, his insistence on the 'inescapable'. The word suggests that whatever this or that image or this or that theatre is capable of provoking, and however we are capable of responding as spectators and as participants, the politics is unavoidable, is bound to come round sooner or later. In the next section, as promised, I look at a particular theatrical example and consider some of the ways in which politics does 'come round', in the world and in the theatre. We take a glimpse too at what is involved in trying to escape one sort of political cycle, a cycle of images and stories and representations, for another sort of politics altogether, a politics of performance that attempts explicitly to step out of the picture.

Theatre

'*One Black actress plays all characters*' (debbie tucker green, *random*, p. 2). March 2008. A young woman comes onto the stage at the Royal Court Theatre in London and starts talking.

> ... And the su'un in the air –
> in the room –
> in the day –
> like the
> shadow of a shadow feeling ...
> off key – I ...
> look the clock. Eyeball it.
> It looks me back.
> Stare the shit down –
> it stares me right back. (p. 3)

She talks, then, like a young black woman, in London perhaps, although no particular city is specified, might be expected to talk when she talks about ordinary things. She tells us about waking up of a morning, same stuff as every morning, although this being the particular morning that she is here to talk about right now, in the hearing of all these people who have paid money to see her and listen to her in the theatre, there is already something extraordinary about all of this ordinary stuff: 'su'un in the air – in the room – in the day'.

There is, though, little else to this theatre other than this actress talking to us, standing there dressed like someone you could see in the street outside, sounding like plenty of people who are in the audience this evening might sound if it were they up there talking. Indeed, for the first twenty minutes or so she may as well be an 'ordinary person', some member of the public who has gone up on stage to tell her story, given that in Sacha Wares's production of debbie tucker green's play *random* – which is what we are here to watch – there isn't even any theatre lighting to intensify her separation from us. There is just the basic, theatrical separation between those of us in the auditorium who have gone there to see a play and this woman on the stage who appears up there in front of us, even as she gets under our skin. Already, though, we might be asking ourselves: appears in front of us as what? As the actress, Nadine Marshall, who plays all the characters? As 'Sister', whose voice opens and closes the play? Or as any of the other characters, 'Brother', 'Mum', 'Dad', 'Teacher', whose voices are woven together in Marshall's monologue?

If something does get under our skin it is as much down to the virtuosity of the performer as she switches from voice to voice without missing a beat as it is to the story that these characters share about a day in the life of this family, a pretty much routine day except that this is the day when Sister's younger brother, Mum and Dad's son, is knifed to death in a 'random' attack on the high street outside the butcher's shop at 1.30 in the afternoon. The entire plot of the play consists of Sister recounting the day's events in her monologue: herself and her brother waking for school, the news of his death being brought to the family home by the police, the responses of the family members and others to what has happened. The effectiveness of the play has to do with a tension between story and performance that has us constantly pulling focus between the one and the other, as I suggested in the discussion of the relationship between a photograph and the scene that it represents. The performance, through which Sister's story is told, belongs to an improvisatory, in-the-moment, thinking-on-the-feet business of verbal back-chat and quick invention, whereas the slow unfolding of the narrative seems like a hopeless attempt to delay the approach of the inevitable. 'We already way too late. / ... And never even knew it' (p. 34). Narrative and performance are, however, woven together in such a way that the audience may not even notice until the show is well under way (it took a while for this member of the audience to notice) that the auditorium *has* been darkened after all, and the stage lights *have* been focused around that strange creature up there who looks and sounds like one of us, giving voice to these stunned testimonies.

She repeats a story that has been told before, countless times, both in the theatre (imagine how many repetitions the actress Marshall has had to go through to achieve this sureness of rhythm, to make this performance something she can carry around with her like a second nature and take onto the stage as 'easily' as that) and in the 'world' that the theatre represents. As Sister puts it: 'Fuck this cycle of shit' (p. 49). This evening, though, on the occasion of Nadine Marshall's performance and our witnessing of that performance, what goes on is also live and unique. And it is something to do with that uniqueness and its relationship to the repeatable – a characteristic, of course, of this or any other theatrical performance – that gets under our skin. Something remains with us that provokes our applause at the end of the show and provokes also the thinking and feeling through which, as the political theorist Louis Althusser proposed many years ago on another theatrical occasion, a 'politics' begins 'searching in me, despite myself, now that all the actors and sets have been cleared away, for the advent of its silent discourse' ('The "Piccolo Teatro"', 1969, p. 151).

If we leave the uniqueness and repeatability of theatrical performance aside for the moment, this is a show that anyway – at a glance – appears to lend itself to a more 'political' reading than others. There is, for instance, in terms of a politics of 'identity', something to be made of the dedication of the main stage of the Royal Court, the home of new writing in London, to the work of a young, black, female writer such as tucker green. In the context of the range of voices, faces, cultures, and experiences that are encountered regularly on the UK capital's main stages, the appearance of this work still has something about it of a democratising – and to that extent political – gesture. The effectiveness of this gesture is evidenced in the fact that a large proportion of the audience this evening are black people, which is not always the case, although I should also say that what can appear as a democratising gesture from one perspective is absorbed into the economics of marketing and what Jen Harvie in *Staging the UK* (2005) calls 'cultural commodification' and the fixing of consumer demographics from another (p. 11). There is something democratising too, however, in the diction of tucker green's script, whose poetry keeps faith with the singularities of human speech, be that the parents' Caribbean dialect or Brother's street slang or the no less singular inflections of the 'white' London speech of Sister's workmate John when he and others turn up at her family's front door (we suspect it is the first time they have been there) to commiserate about her brother's death: 'Nah iss not. We juss wanted you to know. Y'know?' (p. 44). Nor is this a simple matter of democratic consensus; rather, it is an example of stage speech as a site for disagreement and the engagement of voices that do not necessarily speak each other's languages easily, a topic that we shall return to later. There is also something to be made, in any 'political' reading of the show, of the theatrical choices that determine the production, from having one actress play all the characters through the unadorned staging and the everyday clothes and vernacular speech and movements of this actress, all of which sets the conditions for how the show communicates with its audience. These conditions include an exposure of the theatre itself: the bare boards of the stage, the back wall, the spectators at their ease in the un-darkened auditorium, at least at the start of the play. This is all in the best traditions of twentieth-century 'political theatre', where the aim was often to enable the audience to see through the theatrical illusion towards the materials and machinery and labour out of which the illusion is constructed.

Beyond all this there is also something to be said, surely, in political terms, about the play itself and its topicality, by which I mean the fact that it is 'about' something going on in the world that should not be happening, that should be preventable, namely the 'cycle of shit' of 'random' acts of street violence and knife crime in British cities in the early years of the twenty-first century that has taken many, too many, mainly teenage, lives. It is at this point too that an argument with the play's politics – if a play can really be said to *have* 'politics' – could kick in. We note the following: the phrase 'cycle of shit' implies a situation that has gone beyond the possibility of political intervention. Also, the title of the play, *random* ('Random don't happen to everybody. / So. / How come / "random" haveta happen to him?' p. 49), focuses on arbitrary accident and personal grief and indignation, as opposed to contestable acts and negotiable causes. We might also point out how the spoken testimony of the family members, who are all 'already way too late. / ... And never even knew it' (p. 34), wraps up insight and judgement in blindness and helplessness, appearing to put the politics of the situation outside the reach of those most affected by it and with the greatest interest in doing something about it.

None of this weighs against the political *potential* that this exemplary piece of theatre opens up, even if the drama does appear at some level to stage a political defeat, having little enough to offer in terms of either political 'commitment' to a stated cause or organised 'resistance' to a state of affairs, and making no sort of promise at all in terms of political 'efficacy'. That potential is not something that can be explained or critiqued simply through the play's political messages or the production's formal structures. It also depends, in a way that is anticipated by the seemingly improvised and in-the-moment responsive quality of Sister's monologue, upon the unpredictability of the audience's response to what goes on in the theatre: what they are able to make for themselves out of what the theatre gives them to think and feel. This unpredictability of theatrical events is also tied up, I argue, with whatever happens to *remain* of the event, for example in the thoughts and feelings of the audience, as it is passing before us. These remains can be the most trivial and seemingly insignificant thing. Any politics of theatre will have to negotiate this tangle between the unforeseen and the repeating, between the live and the scripted, between what was going to happen and what ends up happening after all.

The play itself will remind us, with its story of the tragic and pointless death of a young man who is son and brother to the other characters in the drama, that what happens in the space of a day can leave a mark on the consciousness – or a 'stink' (p. 50) on the face of the world – that can stay with people for a lifetime. A play, however – and this is an obvious enough thing to say – does not touch us in the same way that a real-life tragedy can touch us, even if the 'same thing' happens in both. The way in which the play happens for us, and leaves its own kind of mark on our consciousnesses, is by inviting us to pay attention to a peculiar type of appearance. This is the appearance of an actor, in this instance Nadine Marshall, a creature who comes before us in the flesh and also, so to speak, wrapped around with language. Not only has she a lot to say for herself, in this play at least, but just by standing there before us she seems already to have a great deal to be said *about* her, which the theatre will persuade us to hear and interpret and care about. An actor is a strange enough creature anyway, in this instance particularly so, being at the same time both one and many: 'a Black actress [who] plays all characters' (p. 2). This is the sort of strange appearance, which, if it is done 'right' – although there's no sure programme for that, just the perpetual experiment of rehearsal and testing out in front of actual audiences – can indeed get under your skin, like an irritant (as Alan Read would have it), where something is felt, at work in the system, before you know what it is or how to deal with it. As I have already suggested, the actor we encounter in this show seems so familiar, so easy to engage with, so human, especially when she steps on stage like that at the beginning or when she comes on again at the end, smiling and easy-going, for her curtain call. What, then, does all that language – in which I include again the language of the theatre, the generic language of stage and proscenium and lights and amplification that *already* wraps around this particular human figure, charging her up with interestingness as she stands there in silence for a split second at the start of the show, even before she starts talking – what does all that language do to a person when she appears before us as an actor? What does it do to a person politically?

One sort of answer would be to say that whatever goes on, politically speaking, depends on you. It depends on you – or it depends on us – because, notwithstanding the best efforts of the globally franchised musicals and other such spectaculars that expect a ready return on their expenditure, theatre remains unpredictable in its effects, given that its effects reside largely not in the theatrical spectacle itself but in the spectators and what they are capable of making of it. No matter how well researched, or rehearsed, or road-tested a production may be, there is no guarantee that its theatrical effects will 'work' in the way they are supposed to or that its carefully constructed political messages will be understood in the ways they are supposed to be understood. Indeed, it may be that the real political value of theatre lies, in part, in this very instability and unpredictability.

A second part of the answer has to do with an issue we were considering earlier around the photograph of the protest in Manaus. There I was trying to suggest that although the photograph by its very nature is removed from the events it represents, it still carries about it some grain of that absent reality. It retains some sort of connection or access to a 'truth' that continues to speak through the image – or the play or the performance – even as the image turns its back on this truth; the way we might think of the feature-less back side of a printed photograph turned towards the ever-receding reality of which it is supposed to be a depiction. I spoke earlier also about the liveness and uniqueness of theatrical performance and the way this is tied up with forms of repeatability. The uniqueness of a live performance may well – as I have been suggesting – get under our skin, but if we continue to feel it there, and if it is going to continue to provoke us to 'think' politically in the way Tracy Davis would have us do, it may be because it carries with it something of the world, something of the world's language, as a reminder of whatever it is we cannot go back to, cannot repeat.

If my formulations here are too general, too universal even, there are several more concrete versions of this idea in tucker green's play. These range from the passages on 'Walkers' breakfast', the crisps and coke that are picked up on the way to school from 'the Asian man shop' and which some are 'diggin [...] out their teet still' as they roll up late to their lessons (p. 16); through the pork chops 'from the white man butchers' going bad in the kitchen as the family take in the news from the visiting police; to the 'stink' in the dead brother's room that is still there at the end of the day even though he himself is not. In all these examples, something is left behind of what happened before, caught in the teeth or in the nostrils or still there in the corner of the eye. A similar effect is produced in the form of the play itself, in the way that the various unnamed and generic 'characters' – Mum, Dad, Sister, Brother – come across as ghost voices, trapped in the story and channelled through Nadine Marshall's monologue. And we are not talking about Walkers' crisps anymore. It is as though, somehow, a few unlucky threads of human being got stuck in the teeth of some machine or other – a sort of 'representing machine' – as they were trying to retreat from the 'cycle of shit' that invades the world of the play. Now they are helplessly on display, up there on the stage, where the machine does its work, churning out its messages, telling the story over and over again.

What has happened here in the theatre – as can happen in any representing machine, such as a photograph or a newspaper or a speech or a television programme – is that something has been shown, something has been said, has been brought into appearance, which might not otherwise be shown or spoken of. Let's say the 'politics' begins right there. However, this bringing into appearance has been done in that complex way the theatre specialises in, which has to do with the ones who are here, who are on the spot, standing in for the others who are not. The ones standing in are the actors and spectators, for example, who turned up this evening to participate in the show, but they are also the characters themselves, whose lives have been ruined, who are standing in for, or representing, all the other people whose lives have been changed in this way. This sort of theatrical complication of the situation gets in the way, then, of any attempt to draw out a more straightforward and easy-to-deal-with politics of familiar messages and quick slogans, such as when the press turn up on the scene after Brother's murder:

> The press
> pressin
> the picturesque for a bite.
> Their blue-eyed reporters
> shieldin their zeal
> for a – 'good', 'urban' story
> stepping into these sides
> askin foolish questions
> soundbitin so-called 'solutions'
> in seconds. (p. 41)

Of course, these 'solutions' are a version of the 'political' also, connected with the sorts of arguments that will circulate in public about the 'knife crime' issue and the state of the 'inner cities' and 'urban' culture, some of which arguments will circulate all the way up to local and national government, where laws get made. However, the phrase 'soundbitin so-called "solutions" / in seconds' also suggests that much of what is involved here is a politics of quick fixes, popular prejudice, and superficial analyses of the situation. The implication of Sister's speech at this point seems to be that a superficial approach to the situation, however political its intentions, may be capable of stopping real politics – the important, difficult, and inescapable business of dealing with what is going on – in its tracks. So it is when she tells us about the press interviewing a teenager on the street, trying to get out of him the story they have already made up in their own minds:

> Feelin brave askin a hard-lookin 'hoodie'
> what he thinks.
> Only to find
> under the cloak of Adidas
> is a brother
> whose eyes don't stop flowin.
> Wet raw with weepin.
> But ... they don't show that bit tho. (pp. 41–2)

Of course, Sister's story about the weeping 'hoodie' who will not be shown on TV because the image fails to fit the stereotype is itself – whatever the justice of the image – a 'political' image held up in front of the story to fix her politics (or tucker green's politics) in place. It is not just the press who are looking for an image that fits their understanding of the story. And just as the press in their way seek to speak 'for' the characters and the situation, so does Sister in her way, as do tucker green and the actress Marshall in theirs. That 'speaking for' continues in the conversations and memories of spectators, and also of course in written commentaries such as this one. These all act upon the story in different ways, and in speaking and standing in 'for' the characters – that is to say, in 'representing' them in one way or another – they also cannot help but stand *in their way*.

I have been arguing throughout this section that the political potential of a theatrical performance, its ability to engage the sort of thinking-through of relations of power that we discussed at the start of this book, is likely to depend upon the complex and unpredictable relationship between the liveness of the theatrical event and everything that event is understood to stand for or represent. Politics, though, is about more than thinking. Determining relations of power also means *acting upon* those relations, in order to change them. Among the forms that this acting can take is what we have been calling representation: again, the process of standing up for, or standing in for, others. The politics of such representation are not straightforward at all. It may be that the politics a piece of theatre provokes, along with the politics it already enacts, will have to do after all with the judgements that any of us are able to make. These will be judgements not simply on the justice or injustice of a represented event but on the justice or fidelity of a representation, as discussed by Read (*Theatre, Intimacy & Engagement*, pp. 196–7). This is not so much a question of empirical realism, in the sense of the fidelity of an image to a depicted scene, where the question would be 'But does it really look like that?' or 'Is that really what happened?' At least it is not only a question of realism. It involves the questions we have been exploring throughout this section to do with the 'justice' of an actor's appearing before us and making her particular claim upon our attention. It concerns the 'fidelity' with which she engages with the task of her performance and concerns also the 'judgements' we make – as spectators, as collaborators in the event – upon the thoughts and feelings that this event has provoked in us.

It may be, as the event proceeds, that we cannot help but remember other people whose voices and stories we invent and repeat in the theatre because they are not able to be here, because they are lost somewhere, or because they do not exist. This too is a 'cycle', a situation of 'relations of power' that we may want to break out of, if only to begin establishing different relations with these others and with ourselves. This is how Sister ends her monologue:

> Close back his
> drawer
> close back his
> door –
> keep his stink in.
> Step down the – too quiet stairs
> past the stank Dad still sittin in
> from the kitchen.
> Pass the socked Support Officer
> struggling –
> in the best room
> with our ...
> my
> destroyed Mum.
> And I ...
> Step out.
> Right.
> Right. (p. 50)

Right enough. That stepping out no longer sounds like normal 'representation'. It sounds like something else, and a different sort of politics altogether: less like a person in a picture with something to 'say' and more like a person breaking right out of the picture, an effect that is underlined by the way the lights go out in the theatre as soon as these words are said. If the lights going off like that make such an action look easy, however, that is the last and the most impressive theatrical illusion of the evening. Action – like thought – is hard work, and that is the topic of the next section.

Work

Theatre and politics, whatever connection they do or do not have with each other, are both hard work. That politics is hard work we probably knew already. The photograph I described at the start of this book indicates the sort of work involved in political activity, not just the violent encounter depicted there but the less immediately 'dramatic' labour behind the picture of education and organisation and argument that goes into any political campaign. It is the sort of distinction touched on by Alan Read in *Theatre, Intimacy & Engagement* when he separates received ideas of 'political theatre' from the 'slower, but harder politics of performance that traces the associations of the social and interrupts the continuity of inequalities, suffering and loss' (p. 272). There are distinctions to be made too about the sort of work we find going on in the theatre.

During the twentieth century various forms of political theatre were often directly engaged with work. This engagement included the complex range of activities that made up the 'workers' theatre movement' in the early part of the century, described by Raphael Samuel, Ewan MacColl, and Stuart Cosgrove in *Theatres of the Left 1880–1935* (1985), and later activist plays depicting the plight of workers and other oppressed groups in a modern capitalist economy. It included too the development of theatrical aesthetics that counter theatrical illusion by exposing the 'workings' of the theatrical operation: the lights, the off-stage areas, the scripts, and so on. It also included a theatrical ethic that privileged the working 'processes' of rehearsal and discovery over the finished spectacle. We shall still ask, however, whether such a basically playful and un-dangerous medium as the theatre could ever justly be compared to the sort of 'real work' involved in certain sorts of politics. One answer is that the assumption behind this question risks ignoring the real danger that theatre-makers, performers, and other artists and writers have faced and continue to face in situations where the irritant potential of the politics of performance is still keenly felt by those with the power to do something about it. Ample evidence of this danger continues to be published on the websites of organisations such as International PEN (www.internationalpen.org.uk), Index on Censorship (www.indexoncensorship.org), and Amnesty International (www.amnesty.org).

We can also, though, pursue the relations of theatre and politics through the topic of work in other ways that continue to respect the theatrical and the political as distinct, if related, arenas of operation. One approach would be that taken by Nicholas Ridout in his 2006 book *Stage Fright,*

Animals, and Other Theatrical Problems, a book with its sights set firmly on material elements that are specific to the experience of theatre but that are often left out of accounts that focus on interpreting what we are supposed to see and hear in a written play or what we imagine we are supposed to notice in a staged performance. These include unintentional, affective elements of the theatre such as actors' stage fright and the tendency to collapse into giggles known as 'corpsing'; or the embarrassment of audiences when they do not know what is supposed to be going on (or when they see all too clearly what is supposed to be going on); or the peculiar fascination that non-human actors such as animals can have for us when we see them on the stage. One of Ridout's arguments is that when these affective elements — these feelings of shame, embarrassment, fascination, and so on which normally we regard as non-essential to our understanding of a show — come to our attention, it is usually because something has gone wrong with the management of the theatrical spectacle. When this happens our attention slips a gear and we find ourselves drawn not so much to what the theatre has to say to us as to its extraneous bits and pieces (an actor's giggles, a mouse running across the stage). At such moments, as Ridout puts it at one point, 'we are simply watching the cogs of the machinery spinning around' (p. 154), marvelling at all of this work going on, and maybe reflecting too on the machinery of work and play and economic dependence, the structures of 'labour' and 'leisure', that drive our lives as workers and consumers. As Ridout writes at the end of his book, '[T]he theatre is, among other things, the place we go to feel what we feel about work and the constraints it places upon our freedom, and certainly not the place we go to experience some a-historical freedom from work, however much it might try to kid us otherwise' (p. 167).

How, though, could it be that the point at which the theatre appears to be working hardest to communicate its message, political or otherwise, should also be the point where the theatre falls apart and shows what it was not supposed to be showing (p. 33), opening up the potential of another, unintended politics of performance that was there all along and is only now set to work or put into play?

It may take some amount of work on our part to get our heads around that, particularly if one of the places we start from is the not unreasonable intuition, again, that the politics we picked up on in the scenes we have encountered so far in this discussion (a factual image of a woman in poverty resisting a line of riot police in a dispute over rights to work the land in Brazil, and a fictional play about a contemporary British family whose son and brother is lost in a meaningless street attack) has to do with immediate, obvious, and indisputable identifications of injustice. It does not take much, really, to make sense of or work out what is going on there, nor is there anything much accidental about the communication. However, if we do take a hint from writers such as Ridout and Read and think about the politics of performance involved in what these and other scenes are *doing*, as well as what we are doing when we take an interest – and even pleasure – in these scenes, then we may consider further what is going on when a theatrical performance works 'for' us in particular ways.

Or, indeed, works 'on' us in particular ways, as a form of political persuasion. A classic locus of these concerns is Shakespeare's *Julius Caesar*, a political play if ever there was one, full of scenes about political and theatrical ways of 'working' on people's sympathies, first staged in London more than four hundred years ago and written towards the end of the reign of Queen Elizabeth I. The first half of the play follows the republican conspiracy against and assassination of the emperor Caesar, and the second half covers the bloody civil war that follows this event. The scene that marks the climax of the play's first half (Act III, Scene II) is not, however, the assassination of Julius Caesar in front of the Senate House, the venue of law-making and government, but the funeral speeches of Brutus, the leader of the conspirators, and Mark Antony, a friend and ally of Caesar's, that are made in the public Forum in front of a crowd of Roman citizens. In the main, the scene functions as a debate between competing politicians, a battle to determine the future governance of the Roman state that will be decided on the basis of which of the two speakers can carry the sympathy of the on-stage crowd. Given that it will, in effect, be decided by the voices — or votes — of the assembled populace, the contest is like a crude or parodic form of democracy. If, that is, we are satisfied with an idea of democracy (in a slave-owning society, where the only people who appear to have a decisive role in public life are men) where the 'parties' and their interests are already known and where the contest is played out between men of power who know how to play the game – the 'game' being one of public speaking, or oratory, that depends on specific, established performance skills and conventions. Anyone who does not accept the terms of this way of speaking is unlikely to be heard from.

The outcome of the scene is well known. The 'noble Brutus' speaks first and speaks well, rationalising the assassination of Caesar in patriotic terms ('Not that I loved Caesar less, but that I loved Rome more') and appealing to the citizens' political interests as 'free' subjects of a renascent republic founded in the ashes of authoritarian rule. Brutus's speech is a success, the crowd is persuaded, and the contest appears to be over before it has begun. But then Antony steps up, bringing with him the bloodied corpse of the assassinated emperor. He works on the crowd piece by piece, addressing them as they would want to be addressed ('Friends, Romans, countrymen'). He claims that he himself has no skills in public speaking, but instead is talking from the heart ('I am no orator, as Brutus is; / But, as you know me all, a plain blunt man'). He claims at one point to be so overcome with grief that words fail him. He claims that he is there only to mourn Caesar and honour the conspirators. And at the same time he insinuates suspicion ('Did this in Caesar seem ambitious?'), playing not to political reason so much as to sentiment ('If you have tears, prepare to shed them now') and, crucially, drawing the crowd's attention to the *picture* of Caesar's corpse, present before them, and to that extent as *moving* as any picture can be ('O piteous spectacle'). There is a pay-off to the speech to do with cash and gardens left to the citizenry in Caesar's will, but by that point the damage is done. Mark Antony's speech has worked its trick, winning the crowd over not through the presentation of far-sighted political reason that Brutus attempted in his speech but through a stirring-up and manipulation of violent emotions and a popular appeal to immediate fears and sentimental attachments (not least attachment to the sight of Caesar's bleeding body and Antony's own performance of the signs of private grief). The crowd are ready to tear the city apart and civil war has begun, the first incident of which is a brief and brutal scene of random street violence in which a poet called Cinna is torn to pieces by a mob for sharing a name with Cinna the conspirator – or maybe for no reason at all.

Mark Antony is a master of persuasion and verbal propaganda. His speech is, in all sorts of ways, in its deployment of a range of emotive triggers, a masterful performance, or at least a gift for a certain sort of masterful actor. This was demonstrated by Marlon Brando in Joseph L. Mankiewicz's 1953 film of the play, made during the time of McCarthyism and the House Committee on Un-American Activities (HUAC) hearings on perceived Communist threats to US 'internal security', a particularly paranoid period in American history at the height of the propaganda cold war with the USSR. Among much that is striking about the scene in Mankiewicz's film version of *Julius Caesar* is the use of a device, the close-up, that is not possible in the theatre without access to specific technology, where the faces of the actors are generally not seen by an audience on the scale we imagine them when we read a play. Close-ups on Brando's face in the film during the choked-up pauses of Antony's speech indicate the extent to which the performance is a calculated political ruse. As spectators of the film we get to watch the character watching – or, more precisely, listening to – the effect that his speech is having on the crowd. We also, of course, get to watch the actor Brando at work. More to the point, we watch the actor's Method at work, register-ing with the slightest shifting of the eyes the effect of 'his' (Brando's or Antony's) performance. This is a performance which involves the persuasion of two sets of intended hear-ers: the fictional Roman crowd on screen, who are, again, persuaded to violent revolt, and the spectators in the cin-ema, who may be persuaded by this display to distance them-selves from what is clearly manipulative in the performance and, presumably, draw a lesson about the dangers of all such charismatic manipulation in the public arena. The two audi-ences at this scene, then, are doing different kinds of work, although both, ultimately, may be doing politics of a sort: both the audience on stage or on screen, whose immediate interests are addressed by the demagogue orator, and the spectators in the auditorium, who are likely to take a more *aesthetic* interest (or even *dis*interest) in this display.

In the Shakespearean scene the orator's performance provokes a public riot that once let slip may be impossible to control. However, the *theatre* audience at this scene are immunised by the fiction of the theatrical situation against the risk of the oratory working on them in the same way.

There will, then, odd as it may seem, be difficulties for any production of the play that attempts to draw 'political' capital out of the drama – not that there have not been many attempts to do so in the four hundred years or so since Shakespeare's play was first performed. One recent example was a lavish 2005 production by the Royal Shakespeare Company at the Barbican, London, directed by Deborah Warner, with a stellar British cast (Fiona Shaw, Ralph Fiennes, Simon Russell Beale, and others) and an explicitly 'political' frame of reference. This frame of reference was evidenced by photographs and statements around the Iraq war in the glossy programme and by the association on stage of the machinations of the political class 'at home' with military operations in some unspecified encampment far away. Most distinctively, the production also featured, in the role of the Roman populace, a group of around two hundred extras recognisably dressed up to represent a range of contemporary 'urban' types. Yet the effect of such a crowd on stage – for this spectator anyway – was to serve as a reminder that however many extras there are, and however authentically stereotyped the postures and the get-up, they can never be enough to turn the theatrical fiction into something other than a theatrical fiction, to turn it into something more 'real'. To achieve that effect the crowd would have to be as large, perhaps, as the actual populace, or large enough for the crowd and the populace to be one and the same. The same goes for the 'realistic' military paraphernalia, the walkie-talkies and combat gear, none of which can ever be realistic *enough* – even with Ralph Fiennes barking out the Mark Antony speech for all he's worth – for the production's apparent claim upon some sort of political engagement to be anything more than that, an apparent claim. Remarkably, where the production was convincing – one suspects unintentionally – was in the case of that stellar cast, who, excellent as they all were, were persuasive not so much through their individual acting skills as at the level of the casting, where the play's political narrative appeared to have been supported by the cultural capital of the British theatre's star system. The professional fame of this group, who have most likely followed each other's reputations for years, who will have known and admired each other's work, who may well have trained in the same institutions, would appear to match, with considerable justice, the private and public sociality of the patrician class that is the main 'character' in Shakespeare's play. The politics of performance, then, in this production had less to do with allusions to the Iraq war than with the genuine estrangement effected in this display of the economics of professional association, and what that association may prove to be worth – commercially, 'culturally' – on the open (theatrical) market.

The persuasive work of the 'actor', whether on the political or the theatrical stage, was approached more explicitly in a late 1990s production of the play, *Giulio Cesare*, by the Italian company Sòcìetas Raffaello Sanzio. Here there was little claim to any contemporary social or political relevance. Rather, the production threw together an esoteric and historically tangled range of references, from the Latin of the Roman orator Cicero, through allusions to Jonathan Swift's eighteenth-century novel *Gulliver's Travels*, to the surrealist iconography of the photographer Man Ray and the painter Magritte, not to mention 'appearances' (visual and vocal) along the way from the likes of Jesus Christ, Stanislavski, and Daffy Duck. What these numerous elements added up to was a complex meditation on voices, faces, and performing bodies and how these function variously in the contexts of theatrical – and political – persuasion and relations of power that are explored in Shakespeare's play. In this show Mark Antony's speech was spoken in a climactic scene just before the interval by a balding and aged actor, Dalmazio Masini. His right arm, like Brando's in the film, was held in the classical outreaching posture of the Roman statues. His voice, though, unlike Brando's or Fiennes's, barely sounded as he performed the speech, as the actor has undergone a laryngectomy. That means he has no vocal chords, and what voice he does have is produced through a clearly visible hole in his throat, filling the theatre with a strange, amplified breathy whisper. Nor was the speech delivered to an onstage crowd, whether of two hundred or two or twenty, but directly to the theatre audience, as if 'we', after all, are the ones this oratory is 'for', as if even after all this time it can still 'work' on us. And by several accounts, among which I would include my own, it does.

That said, the speech is not likely to persuade us in terms of what it actually says. Indeed, by the end it is anyway more cacophony than communication, as the soundtrack from Brando's film performance is added to the audio mix. If the scene is effective in the way it works on us, this may have

41

to do with a theatrical rather than rhetorical effectiveness (if we take rhetoric to refer to the techniques of persuasive speech that Brutus and Mark Antony are so well trained in). Theatrical effectiveness, I suggest – to recall the discussion in the previous section of the work of the actress Nadine Marshall in debbie tucker green's play – has less to do with the linguistic efficiency of speeches and messages than with the unsettling experience of encounter and appearance. When the drama of worldly politics – which is what so much of Shakespeare's play is about – is turned over, as it is in this production, to a focus on how relations of power are organised *in the theatre*, then we might take the opportunity to think of other sorts of politics going on behind the public power-play of speeches and plots and Senate meetings and battlefield tactics and the like. We may think, for example, as I have suggested in earlier sections of this book, about the ways in which politics attaches itself also, as it does in the theatre, to the visibility and vulnerability of particular bodies or to the articulacy and audibility of particular voices, particular languages and gestures.

As I have been proposing throughout this section, theatre can often 'work' – theatrically and politically – at those points where its political messages appear to break down. Shakespeare's play offers interesting examples of moments when the political force of what the actor is *saying* and the theatrical force of what the scene is *doing* would appear to be aiming in different directions, even at different audiences entirely. What I have also been suggesting, however, is that the theatre may be capable of stopping us in our tracks, and deliberately so, with the appearance, in all defiance and fragility, of the actor. That actor is not *necessarily* a human actor. It is, though, likely to be one whom we recognise as caught up in all the paraphernalia and machinery of theatrical representation and, even so, as if over a great distance, claiming some sort of relationship, some sort of community, with us. This is not to say that the theatre, on such occasions, stops in *its* tracks. The cogs of the machinery continue to spin. The theatre continues to do its work. As it does so, however, and as we watch the cogs spin, we register something of what determines relations of power in *this* given space, and perhaps we imagine how those relations could be different.

Pleasure

As we saw in the previous section, one of the key questions raised by Shakespeare's play *Julius Caesar* for a consideration of theatre *and* politics has to do with the workings of rhetoric. I proposed also at the end of the opening section that much of the theatre's value for political thinking may derive – paradoxically perhaps – from 'its seeming fragility and tendency to *un*truth' rather than from the strength of its representations and the justice of its political 'messages'. It may be, now, that the spectacle of manipulative rhetorical speeches being delivered on stage by seemingly fragile performers who draw our attention more to the machinery of representation and amplification than to the words they are actually saying raises some very particular questions about the structures of trust, communication, and political representation that are supposed to govern our lives more generally. How, for example, are we able to trust political speech when we encounter it in the world, in the public life of our democratic societies, when the theatre has shown us that it is possible for speech to be convincing – and to move us emotionally – even when we know its message to be untrue? To get to the roots of such questions we need to go back to a time and place that saw not only the classical birth of dramatic theatre but also arguably the birth of politics as we have come to understand it.

Questions about the political role of theatre in democratic societies have been around since the first recorded 'democracy' in the Athenian city-state two-and-a-half thousand years ago. Just like the later Roman world that lends its history to Shakespeare's play, however, this was a slave-owning society with a restricted measure of equality. The arguments about the social function of theatre that appear in the writings of the two major philosophers of the period, Plato and Aristotle, rich and suggestive as these arguments are, are concerned throughout with what theatre can (and cannot) contribute to the maintenance of this social order.

In Plato's writings considerations of theatrical and other performances pretty much appear only in the context of discussions about political organisation. Of course, theatrical performances staged in massive, permanent, purpose-built theatres at key locations in Greek settlements, during major religious and civic festivals, were a significant part of public life in Plato's and Aristotle's time. Plato acknowledges the enjoyment to be had from theatrical performances.

Furthermore, his key texts, written in dialogue form and usually starring Plato's teacher, the philosopher Socrates, are full of the pleasures and devices of dramatic writing. These pleasures include scene-setting, narrative and poetic diversions, tone of voice, and the delineation of character, as well as a 'dramatic' negotiation among several speakers who approach understanding through the clarification of *mis*understanding, guided by disagreement, persuasion, and the presentation of argument and evidence. That said, the overarching arguments of Plato's dialogues, when performance is under discussion, tend towards pointing out the threat that performances of a theatrical sort pose to a well-ordered society. Indeed, Plato recommends that politics and theatre – and not just theatre that has something uncomfortable to say about political matters – be kept as far apart as possible.

In part, the Platonic argument around the politics of performance has to do with the sort of perversions of political oratory that Shakespeare would later dramatise in *Julius Caesar*. The technique of persuasive and effective speech – or rhetoric – was the key means in ancient Greece for governmental debate, public ceremony, and legal and political negotiations of all sorts. With the development of rhetoric as a valuable freelance skill, however, it could be practised by any persuasive chancer. Once it had been the province of the virtuous and public-spirited citizen, guiding his hearer towards just and true conclusions. Now, a canny orator, as Plato shows us in his book *Gorgias*, can win the day by addressing his hearers' individual and immediate self-interests, either through flattery or through a direct appeal to pleasure, like a sweet-maker conducting a debate with a doctor before an audience of schoolchildren (p. 46, §464). Doing oratory is not the same thing as doing theatre, as we began to explore in the previous section; even so, the appeal to pleasure that Plato's mouthpiece Socrates criticises in *Gorgias* is important to the case that Plato launches against those performances we would recognise as more like actual theatre.

A section of one of Plato's last texts, *The Laws*, in which the speaker admits he may be getting a bit carried away with himself but carries on regardless, rehearses a legend about the decline of Athenian democracy. This decline is pretty firmly marked down to the unpardonable practice of mixing up the types and genres of musical performance, a sort of revolt through mash-up (pp. 107–10, §§700–1). It is a parable about the political force of performance conventions. Once upon a time, according to the legend, particular melodies and rhythms belonged to particular musical genres, and no account was taken of the noisy disapproval – or approval – of audiences, so people of taste would listen in silence while 'children and their attendants and the general public could always be disciplined and controlled with a stick'. Since that time, however, composers 'gripped by a frenzied and excessive lust for pleasure' have assumed a licence to mix up genres, tunes, and the instruments they are played on according to what pleases a member of their audience 'whether he is a good man or not'. The result is that 'democracy' has collapsed into what Plato calls 'a sort of vicious "theatrocracy"', or 'boxofficeocracy' (p. 510): governance by the applauding mob. Or so Plato presents the people who make up the audiences of these performances, who, having developed a taste for getting what they like in the theatre, consider themselves 'an authority on everything' and demand the same response of their political structures.

A case, it would appear, of a surfeit of democracy, which is to be guarded against – as Plato's most extensive discussion of the theatre in *The Republic* has it – by forbidding all theatrical performance from the ideal city-state. It is important to point out what has been pointed out many times in discussions of the case that Socrates makes against the dramatic theatre in Plato's *Republic*: that what is proposed here is not a form of theatrical censorship as we tend to understand that concept. The issue is to do not with particular plays or performances that in some specific way resist the political status quo but with theatre as such and the corrupting influence of the sort of pleasures that are to be found there, that is to say, the political dangers of any theatrical entertainment. At the heart of the argument, which is developed throughout Book X of *The Republic*, are aspects of performance that we have touched on already in our discussion of the 'secondary' nature of the photograph of the confrontation in Brazil and the 'multiple' nature of Nadine Marshall's performance as she 'plays all characters' in debbie tucker green's play *random*. The argument has to do with the fact that the sorts of appearances we encounter in the theatre are essentially representations or imitations, and imitations that do not lead us back to the things that they are imitations of, however much they intend or pretend to, but encourage us to take pleasure in imitation for its own sake.

Poetic imitations, Plato reminds us, appeal to the senses, and also to the pleasures we take when we encounter something that is divided from itself, encouraging us in turn to indulge divisions in ourselves, particularly with regard to those parts – Plato implies that these are the feminine or childish or animal parts – that are supposedly morally fragile and therefore easier to please. For Plato, actorly representation, or *mimesis*, which involves the actor in a division between himself and the character he is imitating or inventing, is a sign of human weakness. It is also a means of provoking weakness in others, and hence a threat to or an infection of the body politic. We remember the film close-ups on Marlon Brando's performance, where the deliberate self-division of both actor and character are made explicit and shown to be the means by which the Roman crowd are persuaded *to* a particular course of political action and by which the cinema audience are persuaded *of* the fidelity of a talented actor's representation of just such a political manipulator. As to what Plato would have made of Nadine Marshall's performance, where a female actor plays all the parts, dividing herself with a seamless virtuosity while at the same time, somehow, remaining integral and present, as singular a presence as you could ask for (and a challenge to our thoughts as to what constitutes a 'virtuous' performance), one dreads to think.

For Plato's pupil Aristotle, the sort of political threat posed by freelance oratory and the seductions of poetry was a danger that could be taken in hand. It had already been taken in hand, he suggests, by tragedy, the dominant dramatic form of the Athenian theatre and a form which, on the strength of the theatrical examples we have been discussing so far, is still going strong in the twenty-first century. Aristotle, in the collection of condensed statements known as *Poetics*, starts from the same basic premise as Plato, the observation that poetic and performing arts, including dancing and 'most flute-playing and lyre-playing, are all, viewed as a whole, modes of imitation' (p. 2316, §1447). Aristotle also aims at the same end as his teacher, a mode of political containment that serves the established order in the city-state. He proceeds, though, by way of a very different set of conclusions.

There is much that is obscure in Aristotle's brief text. Although it puts the emotions at the heart of its theory, specifically the emotions of pity and fear, it is also rather technical and dry in its approach – and, for all that, not necessarily easy to understand. For example, it is a text that can leave us wondering how the rather mysterious experience of emotional processing, or emotional purging, or maybe emotional cleansing, that Aristotle calls 'catharsis' actually works. It is supposed to work through the evocation of those specific emotions of pity and fear (pity for the sufferings of the tragic hero and fear in the face of the dangers that afflict the hero and could also afflict ourselves), and the philosopher does offer a list of the types of stories, or the types of deeds, that are more likely, he says, to produce one emotion than another. There has, though, been a great deal of debate over the centuries about how to interpret such condensed and sometimes mysterious concepts. In short, Aristotle proposes

that the pleasure that humans take in encountering and performing imitations of great deeds — including the genuine
pleasure to be taken in the imitation of deeds that fail or
are interrupted in their movement towards perfection, as
happens in tragedy — is related to the pleasure we take in
learning to perform our own deeds, great or small, as we
make our place in the world. That is, we learn and progress
through pleasure and imitation, instincts that are supposed
to be 'natural' to us and that get to be finely tuned by the
theatre's own highly developed arts of imitation. That fine-
tuning includes a purging, or re-directing or clarifying, of
the destabilising emotions that, as Plato recognised, the theatre specialises in, through a sort of homeopathic action that
is less likely to lead to a change in the political state of things
than to a recognition of those feelings that need to be kept in
check for the sake of the common political good. Theatre, in
this account, would be a means of running off, as if through a
drainage channel or short-circuit, any generative charge, any
static electricity in the politics of performance that threatens
the status quo.

At the heart of Aristotle's account of the way that catharsis is able to channel and nullify all shocks to the social
system is an operation that has haunted 'radical' performance right up to our own day, rendering the most 'trans-
gressive' or 'subversive' art forms, particularly in later
capitalist societies, liable to co-optation by an economic
system that is always able to make room at home and fat-
ten itself upon what pretends to threaten it. We see this in
the constant ability of the cultural mainstream to absorb

and promote influences that only yesterday were being denounced as shocking or threatening to society. That said, taking Aristotle's reading of tragedy in another direction, we can find much of value in a performance form that still has something to teach us about the difficulty of doing good in a world beset by seemingly insuperable evils and 'random' misfortune. And because happiness for Aristotle, as the highest good at which human activity can aim, is bound up in the daily practice of good or virtuous actions, actions based in right reason and steering a course towards moderate and well-balanced behaviour, we learn something too about the difficulties, and challenges, of being happy on this earth. In the face of so much evil in the world we can at times feel defeated even before we begin to think of how to do something about it. In our own time, in the face of particular evils such as global inequality and mass poverty, an increasingly degraded planetary ecology, and an apparently inexhaustible supply of enemies ready to wage war without end, along with the ready co-optation of any form of resistance into another opportunity for the market, it may seem that politics has been exhausted and radicality dug up at the root and scattered for compost. Such a seeming impasse, however, may turn us back to the lessons to be drawn from the complex and uncompromising pleasures we take in tragic imitations.

For a start, tragedy always has a 'case' to make, a singular human case, like a case in court (note all the specific cases of deeds done and consequences suffered that Aristotle proposes from Greek mythology as suitable for provoking the tragic emotions), from which, whatever the 'characters' in the case are or are not able to learn for themselves, there may still be something for the rest of us to learn about how the world goes. As playwright Bertolt Brecht says in *Brecht on Theatre* (1978) of his own tragedy *Mother Courage*, 'even if Courage learns nothing else at least the audience can, in my view, learn something by observing her' (p. 229).

We still have some questions about the forms that this sort of observation can take, questions, I want to suggest now, in conclusion to this section, which can be usefully explored through a consideration of the temporal – and historical – structures of our engagements with theatrical imitation. I said something about this earlier, in the discussion of the liveness of the actor's performance in debbie tucker green's play and how that liveness relates at the same time to structures of temporal repetition. In his book *Performing History* (2007), which deals with plays about tragic events in the past, specifically relating to the Holocaust and the French Revolution, theatre historian Freddie Rokem pursues the theme of theatrical 'imitation' and self-division that so occupied the Greeks. He takes the theme, though, in a particular direction that undermines some of the assumptions we might hold about the 'present tense' of the live theatrical encounter, assumptions that inform how we are able to think about the politics of the theatre event. As Rokem says, '[H]istorical figures who are presented on the stage act in their own time "as if" their deeds were being done in the present, while on the stage their actions are determined by the fact that they represent historical figures who are appearing again' (p. 101). So, for example, a famous figure from the French Revolution, such as Danton, walks about on the stage in front of us seemingly as if his actions and speeches were taking place in the present, and happening live, for this one time only. However, he appears to us, the spectators, as a ghost from a past time who is appearing here not for the first time but, already and ever after, 'again'. In this situation – as we saw with the character of Sister in *random* or the actor who plays Mark Antony in Socìetas Raffaello Sanzio's *Giulio Cesare* – the figure on stage is both a character in the scene and a witness to their own performance, as if they were watching themselves having to go through the motions one more time. It is in this sense that I understand Sister's desire to 'step out' of the scene at the end of her monologue. The audience, then, are also witnesses to the actor's act of witnessing, caught up, to use a term that Brecht offers us, in a sort of estrangement, or *Verfremdungseffekt*. As Rokem says, some theatrical moments 'can bring the spectator to an awareness of seeing oneself seeing the past ... appearing again tonight' (p. 184). In other words, not only is the past remembered in the present, but also a future – the future of the spectators – is somehow made available to these figures from the tragic past. This future is the possibility of a new human relation, a relation to the future of the world that was not available *then* but could be available now, at least as an idea, if only in the theatre. Rokem calls this 'an idea of utopia' (p. 184), which is to say the idea of an ideal place or an ideal social organisation that is unlikely to be found yet in this, or any other, 'given space'.

It is a challenge to imagine how such a political future, a future unimaginable for the figures from other times and other places who haunt our stages every evening, could be represented in the theatre. At the same time, we remember that Plato's *Republic*, in which Socrates argues for banning the theatre from the ideal city-state, is itself in part a utopian vision, although a utopia of a different sort. In Plato's political utopia, as we have seen, theatrical pleasure functions as a disease, a destabilising threat to the status quo. In Aristotle's no less authoritarian political programme the theatre is a means of channelling, or purging, or appropriating, its dangerous emotional material. But this material remains, in a sense, infectious and a destabilising influence on political organisation. As if the theatre still harboured within itself, whatever the political agenda at hand, the constant promise – or threat – of *another* politics. I develop these ideas in the next section, where I consider the ways in which theatre's most familiar structures and functions, not least its function as 'entertainment', have also been a problem for twentieth-century attempts to turn Plato's and Aristotle's formulations around and produce a radical and anti-authoritarian *political* theatre.

Political theatre?

The suggestion that future utopias can be located at the site of a performed *past* leads me to remark that the theatre would appear to be perennially out of time, both with the world it addresses and itself as a mode of address. I say that while acknowledging the immediacy and punctuality of many forms of theatre and performance, among them many forms of 'politically engaged' theatre, from 'Living Newspapers' in Europe and America (discussed by Samuel, MacColl, and Cosgrove in *Theatres of the Left*) and protest theatre in Apartheid-era South Africa during the twentieth century (discussed by Loren Kruger in *Post-Imperial Brecht*, 2004), to the rapid ideological turnover, say, of René Pollesch's work at the Volksbühne in Berlin at the start of the twenty-first. The theme of theatre's slowness or obsolescence is one that keeps coming round, not least since the late nineteenth and early twentieth centuries, when a host of 'radical' practitioners in Europe particularly, from Richard Wagner and August Strindberg to Vsevolod Meyerhold and Bertolt Brecht and Antonin Artaud, sought to overturn theatre practices that no longer seemed appropriate for the modern world – a topic taken up by Raymond Williams in *Drama from Ibsen to Brecht* (1973) and by Peter Szondi in *Theory of the Modern Drama* (1987).

One example of the theme is an argument that playwright and theatre-maker Bertolt Brecht sets out in his *A Short Organum for the Theatre* (1948), a theoretical treatise written towards the end of his career and later reprinted in *Brecht on Theatre*. Brecht begins the treatise by reiterating a theme we have already touched on with Plato and Aristotle – and which has been crucial for just about every Western theatre commentator in the two millennia since – namely, the issue of pleasure and entertainment. For Brecht the theatre is nothing if not pleasurable. 'Let us treat the theatre as a place of entertainment,' he writes. 'It is the noblest function

that we have found for "theatre".' 'Nothing needs less justi-
fication than pleasure.' 'To ask or accept more of the theatre
is to set one's own mark too low' (pp. 180–1). Inevitably,
there is a 'but' following. What follows is the quintessen-
tially modernist claim that the available forms and functions
of entertainment no longer work for 'us', where 'us' is the
transnational community of citizens of industrialised capital-
ism. 'Our whole way of appreciation is starting to get out of
date,' he writes, although what is out of date about it is not so
much the fact that the theatre entertains but that it no longer
entertains to any productive end (p. 183).

This theme of theatre's being out of time continues
beyond Brecht's period. We find it, for example, in 'Street-
Theater and Theater-Theater', a text by the Austrian playwright and novelist Peter Handke written in 1968. This was
a period during which for many, and not just in the West, it
appeared that forms of political revolt were about to make
all sorts of utopias, and all sorts of nightmares too as it happened, not just visible but tangible. For Handke, Brecht is a
figure who has left a strong example from which much can be
learned ('Brecht helped to educate me') but an example that
is fatally compromised by his having worked his instructive
'models of contradiction' through, of all places, the theatre
(pp. 311–15). As a result, Brecht 'never unsettled anyone
who was settled, but he did give countless people a few lovely
hours'. There is that entertainment thing again, although
clearly not entertainment enough, or not the right sort of
entertainment, for the young author. Handke's problem, as
is the way with these things, is not with what the theatre

says, its statements, its declared intentions. He has no problem with Brecht's Marxism, for instance; indeed, he is rather sympathetic to that. What he objects to is theatre's tendency as a 'meaning-making space', as he puts it, to take 'whatever is serious, committed, definite, and final outside the theatre, [and turn it] into a *play* – so that earnestness, commitment, etc., in the theatre are hopelessly subverted by the play-ful and meaning-making context in which they are presented – when will people finally notice this?' (p. 312).

The problem, in short, is that theatre's instrumentalism, its use as a means of guiding our actions and changing the world, does not work – never did, never will. 'The theatre as a social institution strikes me as a useless instrument for the transformation of social institutions,' Handke writes (p. 313). This theme has been picked up by others in our own times, from theorist and theatre-maker Mike Pearson in *Theatre/Archaeology* (2001, co-authored with Michael Shanks) on the limitations of 'hectoring' agit-prop (p. 102) to Forced Entertainment director Tim Etchells on 'the suspect certainties of what other people call political theatre' in *Certain Fragments* (1999, p. 19). Noticeably, though, neither of these theatre-makers is shy of social, or indeed political, engagement. Pearson, for example, writes in that same passage about the possibilities of a 'political theatre' that would give hearing to authentic voices of dissent, challenge the victories of the powerful, extend the range of popular culture, and contribute to local self-determination.

Oddly enough, Handke's next move in the 1968 essay is not to give up on 'politically committed theatre' but to relocate it. Theatre is to be taken out of the *theatres* ('those falsifying art rooms', p. 313) and into the streets, into churches, into shopping malls, and into reappropriated lecture halls. Handke's description of university professors peering blinkingly through smashed doors, leaflets fluttering down from the balconies, revolutionaries carrying their small children with them to the speaker's podium, and so on may strike a nostalgic note now in some places, but presumably it was rousing enough when it was written. The movement of theatre into streets and shopping malls was performed in many places during this period in an attempt, as Bradford D. Martin describes it in *The Theater Is in the Street* (2004), a book on politics and popular performance in 1960s America, to 're-enchant politics' by weaving politics, art, and life together in the same braid. This was a time, according to Living Theatre's Judith Malina, when 'we thought we were going to change everything' (quoted by Martin, p. 13). It was a time of tactical raids on settled assumptions and sensibilities; of taking theatre and performance into non-traditional venues; of collective creation and theoretical discussion; of critique of the money system and the whole 'entertainment' economy of commodity production, alienating spectacle, and uncritical consumption. It was a time when subtle and complex critiques of theatre's political instrumentality were already well developed, as several important discussions since of theatrical activism and cultural politics testify, including Elin Diamond's *Performance and Cultural Politics* (1996, pp. 3–4) and Sue-Ellen Case and Janelle Reinelt's 1991 edited collection *The*

Performance of Power. It was also a time when many hoped that culture (for example, theatrical culture) could serve at the very least as a 'rehearsal for politics' or even, in Handke's more idealistic vision, a 'leap in reality', until 'reality itself has become a single space dedicated to play. That would be beautiful' (p. 314).

Beautiful certainly, although it would still leave the theatre – the 'theatre-theatre' as Handke calls it – out for the count. This is pretty much the position rehearsed in Baz Kershaw's book *The Radical in Performance* (1999). There the political limitations of what Kershaw calls the 'theatre estate' and its 'disciplinary system', which would include the terminal gasps of 'political theatre', are diagnosed in detail. Kershaw focuses on the theatre's spatial-architectural modes of authority and domination, its hierarchised social structures, its exclusionary mechanisms, its unacknowledged value systems, and its tacit commitments – at the very heart of theatrical procedures – to forms of un-freedom. His book rehearses, then, a move which seems to have been played out whenever a renewed hope for 'radical' performance has been at stake, a move in Kershaw's terms 'beyond theatre' – certainly beyond 'political theatre' – but a move too which cannot help but take theatre (and theatrical politics) with it in some form or other.

Brecht in his day was happy enough to take the theatre with him, still confident that the theatre could take in hand the representation of social relations in a way that was entertaining enough – for 'now' – to strike the spark of something new out of the old magic. Hence Brecht's 'method' of estrangement, or *Verfremdung*, which involved showing up as historical (and therefore changeable and renewable) what tend to be encountered as 'naturalised images' in the sense in which I used that phrase in the first section of this book: images that we take as representations of how things are or should be. This estrangement involved dealing with contemporary times 'as though they were historical', as he says in *Brecht on Theatre* (p. 190), thereby establishing the now as a thing of distance and peculiarity. Or else putting figures on stage who are 'not quite identical' to those who are identified with them. 'Imagine,' Brecht proposes, 'a man standing in a valley and making a speech in which he occasionally changes his views or simply utters sentences which contradict one another, so that the accompanying echo forces them into confrontation' (p. 191). Or else, notably, developing the actor's work as a way of 'showing' the differences between the feelings of the character and whatever *other* feelings the actor has (p. 193).

These techniques might strike us, at first glance, as anything *but* 'faithful representations', to recall another idea from earlier in this book. The fidelity, though, after all, *is* to theatrical showing as such. As Jameson argues in *Brecht and Method*, what Brecht's method amounts to is 'the showing of showing, the showing of how you show and demonstrate' (p. 91) rather than any specific didactic content. This method is what Jameson calls the basic pedagogy, or teaching, of Brecht's method of *Verfremdungseffekt*, or V-effect: an effect which is itself, of course, historicisable, and not even *necessarily* 'political' (p. 40). As ever, it depends.

It depends in large part, as I have been suggesting, on how we deal with theatre's temporal and historical aspects, even if all we have left behind by the passing of theatrical time is, in Jameson's words, the 'after-images' of its 'embodied storytelling' (p. 27), its way of physically 'acting out' the things it has to show and say. Indeed, the Brechtian V-effect is singular in all its manifestations and as *historical* as the theatre itself. So, for example, a theatrical device such as the use of a prop, or an actor's gesture or way of speaking, is not only specific to the story being told in that performance; it is also specific to the ways of understanding and cultural frameworks of the audience who were there on that particular evening. It may also, potentially, serve to describe a *condition* of the theatre itself. That is to say, the theatre – and by that I mean any theatre at all – becomes 'estranged' and takes on the peculiarity of an unlikely and dubious occurrence just as soon as we share our after-images with each other, just as soon as we tell someone what was 'really' going on there when we went to see a show.

What, after all, is there to say? We tell our friend that the theatre is a place where people come and go, obsessively it would seem, through the same exposed rooms and spaces (they have been coming and going across the same exposed space of the Royal Court in London for decades), and where they perform various harmless and inconsequential actions: a bit of wandering around, some waving of the arms, some standing up and sitting down, and playing it all up as they do so, often getting remarkably excited. It is a place too, we tell our friend, where every action that is performed appears planned out or scripted in advance, at least to an extent. This produces a strange effect, we say, in that the people who are coming and going across the space – let's call them the actors – seem to have all the freedom in the world to do whatever they like, even the freedom not to do anything at all. But at the same time they seem constrained, as if all their choices are somehow being made for them somewhere else, and as if every move they make is basically a renewed attempt to deal with this peculiar situation.

We see some of these possibilities of the theatre's fundamental estrangement effect being explored in Peter Handke's late play from the 1990s *The Hour We Knew Nothing of Each Other*. If we do not have here the forceful 'political' estrangement of the Brechtian method of dis-illusion (Loren Kruger's translation of *Verfremdung*), the play nevertheless shows something of how the theatre's basic 'setting apart' of human activity contributes to the making and unmaking of theatrical illusion. Handke's wordless play involves thirty or forty actors, in various group combinations, with constant changes of wigs and costumes and props, crossing the stage between the on and the off. And that is all that happens. It seems, though, during the two hours of the play's duration, that several hundred individual characters appear in the small town square that the stage 'represents', even if this illusion is only enabled by a particular arrangement of scenic conventions. The three hundred or so 'characters', in a sort of pre-emptive riposte to the laboured intentionality of the on-stage crowd of the RSC production of *Julius Caesar* discussed earlier, are themselves only a passing effect of the theatre's inescapable aboutness; that is to say, the fact that it is always representing, always standing in for something.

This is what Jameson would call the theatre's 'allegorical' potential (p. 122). Allegory, at a most basic level, has to do with an appearance or a meaning which is also *supposed* to be taken as *something else*. It is a different sort of procedure to metaphor, which has to do with a movement from the familiar to the unfamiliar so as to enable a better understanding of things we do not know. Allegory, in a sense, has to do with the things that we think we know and recognise already seeming oddly insufficient or unconvincing. They do so because we suspect there is another meaning involved, that these representations are standing in for some other thing. In this situation it is often we – as readers or spectators – who contribute this other meaning, indeed heaping all sorts of meanings upon figures who may only, after all, be walking across the stage, carrying a potted plant or opening an umbrella. Handke's play, then, is one in which the potential of *any* appearance to bring with it an allegorical charge is explored exhaustively. Any figure who comes on stage, however briefly, can be taken 'for' a character that I imagine. At the same time, no 'actor' who crosses the stage and no 'character' who crosses the square is necessarily any more or less interesting or significant than any other, and any of them is capable of generating a singular stand-out interest. There is a sort of equality among the representations which, I hasten to note, can only be produced on stage not by taking things for granted or just showing them 'as they are' but through the carefully judged work of all the actors, along with the director and designer and author and other members of the production team, with respect to the estrangement of the stage. And that is not an easy business. Although I would continue to argue that Handke's play – at least as I am trying to describe it here, in an ideal staging of my own imagining – exploits the theatre's fundamental V-effect in an exemplary way, it is not so straightforward to realise that effect in an actual staging in a real theatre. A recent professional production I saw at the National Theatre in London in February 2008 seemed, in various ways, to lose its nerve over the play, building up a level of character-based and situational realism that arguably made this very long and very silent play easier for its audience to get involved with and follow. In doing so, however, the production seemed to lose sight of that unsettling hour 'in which we knew nothing of each other' that the play's title reflects upon, in which the performers might not be *acting* at all, and which points to the fundamental effect of allegorical ambivalence that is capable of infecting *any* theatre and turning the best intentions – be they political intentions or any other sort – inside out. If at the start of this book we considered politics as having to do with determining the 'relations of power in a given space', then we might want to suggest now that Handke's late twentieth-century, and on the face of it *non*-political, play, with its rather generalised form of estrangement, offers us after all a way of thinking about the possibility of a politics – at least in the theatre – of *non*-relation. Could the hour in which we presume to know nothing of each other offer us moments when we might learn to notice each other, outside our relationships to each other, as if for the first time?

In this section I have been suggesting that a sense, at least in modern times, of theatre being out of time with its moment has been an important contributor to a set of movements of 'political' theatre and performance *out of* the theatre, or *beyond* theatre. As if theatre's political potential could be realised only by somehow stepping away from the conventions – indeed the whole outmoded machinery – of theatrical representation. At the same time, I have been arguing that theatre's untimeliness and tangled temporalities are vital factors in the sorts of estrangement of consciousness, the distancing of attachment, and the looking again as if seeing for the first time that inform any engagement in the politics of performance, theatrical or otherwise. A question to ask now, to conclude this section and look ahead to the final part of our discussion, concerns the nature of our engagement with theatre's more untimely and uncomfortable appearances – for example, Brecht's man in the valley speaking contradictory sentences to the valley walls so that the echoes will force these statements into confrontation with each other. I wrote at the opening of this section about 'entertainment', a word that usually refers to the production of amusement and pleasure. Another, related, meaning of that word is to show hospitality to someone, to make them your guest, to hold them in your welcome in the way you might hold an idea in your mind. I think again of those figures in Handke's play, crossing the stage from darkness to darkness, in that hour when we knew nothing of each other but when each of us was exposed to the outside air of other people's attention. I ask myself, now, what it means to 'entertain' the stranger, to entertain a relationship with those others who appear to us as those we know nothing about. Does the stranger – with the 'hospitality' meaning in mind – demand a place among 'our' concerns? And if so, how are we to answer that demand? Or else, if we understand entertainment in its other sense, do these strangers appear only to amuse us from a distance? I like to think of these dual meanings informing Brecht's statement in *Brecht on Theatre* of what 'theatre' consists in: 'making live representations of reported or invented happenings between human beings and doing so with a view to entertainment. At any rate that is what we shall mean when we speak of theatre, whether old or new' (p. 180).

Stubborn messengers

After this consideration of Handke's wordless play, now might be a good moment to recall that for Aristotle (who, as we have seen, also had something to say about the political function of theatre) the possibility of politics was based in the fact that human beings are animals capable of meaningful speech. It is our capacity to do more than make inarticulate cries among one another when we experience pleasure and pain that distinguishes humankind, as 'political animals', from the bees and other sociable life-forms. We are also, says Aristotle in *Politics*, capable of saying something about our feelings and speaking about what should be done and the justice or otherwise of the situations we find ourselves in. It is this capacity for language, too, that enables us to organise among ourselves for the greater social good, to collaborate in the building of societal units – the family, the state, and so on – and to bond with others in the administration of justice, which is 'the principle of order in political society' (pp. 1987–8, §1253a).

Several challenges have, inevitably, been offered to these ideas since *Politics* was written. Both the intention of human beings towards the 'good' and the 'justice' of Aristotle's social model have been questioned by thinkers who would see humankind (even modern, 'enlightened' humankind) as less distinct from the 'brutish' world than all this would imply. The Aristotelian distinction between the political *bios* of humankind and the merely biological *zoe* of other animal life-forms has been brought sharply into focus by the sort of considerations provoked by modern bio-politics, where life itself, its processes and the very conditions of existence of living beings, have been subject to political control. This has been particularly evident during the past century, with millions of speaking beings cast outside the political pale to suffer and be killed – as it were, like animals – with impunity.

This conception of humankind as the speaking animal would, at any rate, appear relevant to the sort of politics we imagine going on in the theatre. This is especially true if we consider the work done by Brecht and other theatre-makers in pitching their representations of social relations on the fault-lines between things that are done (and are shown to be done) and what can be *thought* or *said* about what is shown and done. It is, after all, in the cracks between action and the theorisation of action (which means seeing things through as much as thinking them through) that uncommon values can be revealed in common activities, exposing the causes and contradictions of otherwise seemingly natural processes. From this perspective, what would appear to be at stake for both politics and theatre are the very activities of showing and saying through which some are made visible who would otherwise have 'no business' being seen and others get to speak who would not, in 'normal' circumstances, count as speaking beings. As the long and complex philosophical debate over animal rights has shown, even humans have been coming round to the recognition that we are not the only inhabitants of the planet whose 'rights' should be recognised if the happiness, let alone the survival, of all is to be ensured.

The question of who counts as participating in the 'social' involves not only relations among the larger collective of actors – human and non-human – that make up the world but also divisions among speaking beings themselves. We have already noted that not everyone in the Greek citystate enjoyed the same level of participation in democratic politics. Aristotle himself insisted on an irresolvable division between the rich and the poor (p. 2109, §1329a). This is the sort of division that has to do not just with the distribution of material goods but also, as theatre history teaches us, with the distribution of 'good speaking parts' and the likelihood of having one's voice listened to, or understood, in the wider political drama.

Many of the questions we are gathering here, around issues of political participation and the recognition of each other's linguistic acts as meaningful speech, are explored in the work of the Brazilian theatre-maker, theorist, and political activist, and developer of the techniques of 'image theatre' and 'forum theatre', Augusto Boal. These techniques developed in the early 1970s, as Boal recounts in his book *Theatre of the Oppressed* (1979), out of a literacy programme in Peru among the poor and disadvantaged. For Boal 'the theatre', like language, 'is a weapon. A very efficient weapon' that can be taken in hand by the powerful as a 'tool for domination' just as easily as it can be appropriated by the poor (or whoever is oppressed, whatever the grounds of their oppression or exclusion from society) as 'a weapon of liberation' (p. ix). Thus, Boal does invest in the instrumentality of theatre in the field of politics, although we would want to add immediately that he has spoken of the possibility of *any* sort of theatre — not just the models that he has worked with — effecting a change among the various actors and spectators who are its participants.

Crucial for Boal to the theatre's instrumentality are the ways in which theatre functions 'as language', which is to say as a language 'capable of being utilised by any person, with or without artistic talent. We tried to show in practice how the theatre can be placed at the service of the oppressed, so that they can express themselves and so that, by using this new language, they can also discover new concepts' (p. 121). Key to this practice is forum theatre, where a theatrical scenario, most likely on a topic that directly touches

the lives of the actors and spectators who are involved in the forum, is presented in such a way that the spectators have the opportunity to intervene in the scenario as 'spect-actors': to propose alternative arguments and plot developments and, crucially, to step into an actor's part so as to take the drama in a direction informed by their own understanding of the situation.

Certain things would appear to follow in Boal's thought and practice from this key idea of theatre 'language' and its transferability. One is the transformation – Boal would say the 'humanising' – of the spectator in the forum, who participates in the represented action as 'an actor on an equal plane with those generally accepted as actors, who must also be spectators'. Thus the spectator has 'restor[ed] to him [sic] his capacity of action in all its fullness' (p. 155). This is also, though, where the practice comes up against difficulties, particularly where the spect-actor's participation depends upon agreement not only over shared languages but also over what counts as a 'real' social relation. These are the sorts of difficulties that another practitioner-theorist who has done work among the poor and disadvantaged, Rustom Bharucha, brings out in *The Politics of Cultural Practice* (2000), a book that sets itself in the thick of the complex disagreements (conditions of recalcitrance, un-civility, and non-reciprocity) that determine the contemporary 'globalised' political economy. Although he does not refer directly to Boal, Bharucha recalls theatrical workshops he has been involved in where, even as the victimised and oppressed adopt and adapt theatrical languages to present themselves as 'sites of political evidence', forms of violence are seen to erupt in the work that are so severe as to 'challenge the language of theatre'. As Bharucha himself goes on to add: 'None the less, if such moments of violence challenge the language of theatre, they are points of reference that compel us to inscribe our difficulties in attempting to represent the unrepresentable' (p. 107).

We can argue, anyway, that a Boalian technique such as image theatre, in which 'my conception of "revolution" will become clear if, instead of speaking, I show with images what I think' (p. 138), harbours within it a notion of 'challenged' communication. That is to say, Boal's idea of theatre as language does not presume that all forms of communication, even the basic operations of verbal exchange, are equally available to all. Even so, the emphasis on communication, whether through words or images, might still be politically problematic if what is meant by communication is ultimately a 'clean' and uninterrupted transmission of information from one place to another: from the place of the actor's thoughts, say, to the place of the spectator's understanding. As we have already seen – whether in the philosophical reflections on theatrical *mimesis* among the ancient Greeks, or in the theatrical perversion of oratorical persuasion that we found in various performances of Shakespeare's most famous Roman play, or in the estranged seeing promoted by Brecht, or in Boal's theatre of intervention and debate, or in the way that the most direct and unadorned telling of a story in debbie tucker green's *random* is also a complex, ghostly channelling of 'all characters' – theatrical communication is hardly likely to be that simple.

Nor would we want it to be. As Claudia Castellucci, one of the founder members of the theatre company Socìetas Raffaello Sanzio, whose work I discussed earlier, writes in *The Theatre of Socìetas Raffaello Sanzio* (2007): '[C]ommunication today has become the principal vehicle for political consensus' (p. 217). One implication of this statement is that theatre's job, politically speaking, is to oppose the current state of consensus by provoking disagreements of various sorts. Of course, theatre can never immunise itself from the sorts of languages it shares with the technologies of political domination and social division, as pointed out by Handke and Kershaw. What it may be able to do, though, perhaps along lines proposed by the philosopher Jacques Rancière, who in 'Ten Theses on Politics' (2001) imagines political argument as 'the construction of a paradoxical world that relates two separate worlds', is to imagine these other, paradoxical worlds. Which means also to construct real images of these other worlds. As Claudia Castellucci insists: 'Always and no matter how: another world' (p. 182). That would be another world that, however brief, however virtual, and however fictional (the brief, the virtual, and the fictional are, after all, equally capable of exerting a memorable force), takes its place in this world: if only during that hour or so in the theatre when we are reminded of how little we know of each other.

The ways in which theatre imagines other worlds that contradict this world include the sort of political project proposed by Brecht and others, where theatre's contribution to politics involves interrupting whatever is taken for granted as the 'political' and giving form to the *new*. That said, we do not presume that the sort of new that the theatre is capable of producing is not also something very old come around to make its demands on us again. These demands range from the still unresolved 'cycle of shit' of pointless violence to the still unredeemed sufferings of the poor and destitute. They are demands that may very well *not* be couched in terms of justice and goodness, or not in obvious ways, and that pose challenges as to how any such demand is to be 'communicated' and how it should be answered in return.

As for theatrical communication, and by way of a conclusion to some of the themes I have been discussing concerning other worlds and times, political messages, and our sometimes unsettling and often moving encounters with the messengers themselves, I am reminded of a short text by the science writer Arthur C. Clarke. Clarke's text appears in a 'personal anthology' of essential reading called *The Search for Roots* (2001) put together towards the end of his life by the scientist, author, and Auschwitz survivor Primo Levi. Clarke, in an essay that Levi describes as not trying to describe the future but as defining 'the boundaries within which possible futures must lie' (p. 188), is discussing the popular science fantasy of teleportation. That is the fantasy of being able to transport oneself from one place to another at the push of a button, without the trouble of making a journey. Clarke points out that this particular fantasy is based on a misconception, in that it would not be bodies that were transported in such a system but information about bodies: a system, he says, not unlike television, where it is not the actors who appear on our screens but information about an image or flow of images, processed and 'communicated' through the televisual medium. Furthermore, as Clarke is at pains to demonstrate, 'there is a universe of difference' between a completed image of a man 'and the man himself', and there is no foreseeable future in which our efforts to close that gap will ever be over and done (p. 191).

To illustrate his point Clarke imagines television – the transmission of 'high-definition' images – as it might have been invented by Leonardo da Vinci with the technology available to him in his time. Imagine someone seeking to send information about an image to someone visible in the distance, on the other side of a square, say, or on a far hill. What that person could do is divide the image to be trans-mitted into a grid of squares and use a messaging system such as semaphore or flashing lights to indicate to the other person which of the squares were dark and which were light. The other person, then, could transfer this information to a second, blank, gridded sheet, although it becomes obvi-ous – however fine the grids and however many operators are involved – that the image reproduced at the receiving end is likely, as Plato would have pointed out, to be a crude and indistinct version of the original image.

The system, that is to say, is thick with interference. To which we add for ourselves – if we imagine, say, semaphore as the means of transmission – that an inordinate amount of flag-waving labour would have to be involved in this other-wise simple, and simply ineffective, act of communication.

So much so that the performance of the communicative act and all of its pathos – like Antonin Artaud's image in *The Theatre and Its Double* (1958) of the actor as a victim tied to a burning stake signalling through the flames – may, after all, make up the only image that remains, stubbornly, from all this business. In this image the actors will be waving still, transmitting nothing beyond the act of transmission itself, but in doing so – as another contemporary thinker, Giorgio Agamben, expressed the idea in *The Man without Content* (1999) – 'giv[ing] back to man, who has lost his ability to appropriate his historical space, the concrete space of his action and knowledge' (p. 114).

At this point the proto-televisual system starts looking a little like theatre, where the 'message' and its transmission may never have as much to say to us as the renewed image of those performing bodies crossed by language and linked by the distance that separates them, from each other and from ourselves. Their language will not suffice to share what they need to share with each other. Their speech is tantamount to silence. They are performers whose politics is something that we – imaginary witnesses to the scene in an unimaginable future – know nothing about but whose rigorously intentional gestures, concerned as they are with making the invisible visible, may be worth our taking an interest in.

further reading

The key recent texts to have informed this book are probably 'Theatricality and Civil Society' (2004) by Davis, *Brecht and Method* by Jameson (2000), and *Theatre, Intimacy & Engagement* by Read (2007). Each, in its own different and nuanced way, focuses on relations *between* theatre and politics rather than on political theatre as such. These three texts are a demanding read, but they are packed with a wealth of provocations towards further thought. For some of the key early arguments on theatre *as* politics I recommend the foundational essays by the theorists Adorno ('Commitment'), Benjamin (*Understanding Brecht*), and Althusser ('The "Piccolo Teatro"'), all three of whom also reflect in challenging ways upon the legacy of Brecht. For the views of a contemporary philosophical writer on what the theatre may lend to politics see the work of Rancière, particularly his essay 'The Emancipated Spectator' (2007). Even earlier arguments than those just cited are put forward by Plato and Aristotle. The concerns of these Greek philosophers are still current, and Plato in particular is a very enjoyable read. I recommend starting with Book X of *The Republic*. Excellent book-length studies by scholars in theatre and performance studies that focus explicitly on political ways of thinking about theatre, and on theatrical approaches to political engagement, include *Presence and Resistance* (2004) by Auslander, *Theatre and the World* (1993) and *The Politics of Cultural Practice* (2000) by Bharucha, and *The Politics of Performance* (1992) and *The Radical in Performance* (1999) by Kershaw. The focus of these writers is largely on contemporary practice and current political concerns, whether framed in relation to the 'postmodern condition', the challenges of globalisation, or shifting ecologies of radical and collective action. The same is the case with the collections *Performance and Cultural Politics* (1996) edited by Diamond and *The Performance of Power* (1991) edited by Case and Reinelt, both of which again are explicitly concerned with politically informed and motivated approaches to theatre and performance study and practice. More recent volumes, which I have benefited from greatly, and which exemplify the subtlety and originality of a range of politically inflected writing in current theatre studies are *Talking to the Audience* (2005) by Escolme, *Staging the UK* (2005) by Harvie, and *Stage Fright, Animals, and Other Theatrical Problems* (2006) by Ridout. Many more books and essays could be listed, not only by critics and scholars but also by practitioners. Although my own book seeks to guard against any overoptimistic collapsing of theatre into politics and politics into theatre, it allows that the ways in which these terms face each other and touch on each other's territories are manifold and inexhaustible. Any of the texts listed here will be able to lead readers into their own landscape of thought, through connections with other writings and performances.

Adorno, Theodor W. 'Commitment.' *Aesthetics and Politics*. Theodor W. Adorno, Walter Benjamin, Ernst Bloch, Bertolt Brecht, and Georg Lukács. Trans. Ronald Taylor. London and New York: Verso, 1977. 177–95.

Agamben, Giorgio. *The Man without Content*. Trans. Georgia Albert. Stanford, CA: Stanford UP, 1999.

Althusser, Louis. 'The "Piccolo Teatro": Bertolazzi and Brecht – Notes on a Materialist Theatre.' *For Marx*. Trans. Ben Brewster. Harmondsworth, UK: Penguin, 1969. 129–51.

Aristotle. *Poetics*. *The Complete Works of Aristotle*. *The Revised Oxford Translation*. Vol. 2. Ed. Jonathan Barnes. Princeton, NJ: Princeton UP, 1995. 2316–40.

———. *Politics*. *The Complete Works of Aristotle*. *The Revised Oxford Translation*. Vol. 2. Ed. Jonathan Barnes. Princeton, NJ: Princeton UP, 1995. §1253a. 1986–2129.

Artaud, Antonin. *The Theatre and Its Double*. Trans. Mary Caroline Richards. New York: Grove, 1958.

Auslander, Philip. *Presence and Resistance: Postmodernism and Cultural Politics in Contemporary American Performance*. Ann Arbor: U of Michigan P, 1994.

Benjamin, Walter. *Understanding Brecht*. Trans. Anna Bostock. London: Verso, 2003.

Bharucha, Rustom. *Theatre and the World: Performance and the Politics of Culture*. London and New York: Routledge, 1993.

———. *The Politics of Cultural Practice: Thinking Through Theatre in an Age of Globalization*. London: Athlone, 2000.

Blau, Herbert. *To All Appearances: Ideology and Performance*. London and New York: Routledge, 1992.

Boal, Augusto. *Theater of the Oppressed*. Trans. Charles A. and
    Maria-Odilia L. McBride. London: Pluto, 1979.
————. *Hamlet and the Baker's Son: My Life in Theatre and Politics*. Trans.
    Adrian Jackson and Candida Blaker. London and New York:
    Routledge, 2001.
Bogad, Lawrence M. *Electoral Guerrilla Theatre: Radical Ridicule and
    Social Movements*. London and New York: Routledge, 2005.
Boon, Richard, and Jane Plastow, eds. *Theatre Matters: Performance and
    Culture on the World Stage*. Cambridge: Cambridge UP, 1998.
Brecht, Bertolt. *Brecht on Theatre*. Trans. John Willett. London: Methuen,
    1978.
Carlson, Marvin. *Performance: A Critical Introduction*. 2nd ed. London and
    New York: Routledge, 2003.
Case, Sue-Ellen, and Janelle Reinelt, eds. *The Performance of Power:
    Theatrical Discourse and Politics*. Iowa City: U of Iowa P, 1991.
Castellucci, Claudia, Romeo Castellucci, Chiara Guidi, Joe Kelleher, and
    Nicholas Ridout. *The Theatre of Societas Raffaello Sanzio*. London and
    New York: Routledge, 2007.
Clarke, Arthur C. 'TV According to Leonardo.' *The Search for Roots: A
    Personal Anthology*. Primo Levi. Trans. Peter Forbes. London: Allen
    Lane, 2001. 188–94.
Collini, Stefan. 'On Variousness; and on Persuasion.' *New Left Review* 27
    (2004): 65–97.
Davis, Tracy C. 'Theatricality and Civil Society.' *Theatricality*. Eds. Tracy
    C. Davis and Thomas Postlewait. Cambridge: Cambridge UP, 2004.
    127–55.
Davis, Walter A. *Art and Politics: Psychoanalysis, Ideology, Theatre*. Ann
    Arbor: U of Michigan P, 2007.
Diamond, Elin. ed. *Performance and Cultural Politics*. London and New
    York: Routledge, 1996.
Escolme, Bridget. *Talking to the Audience: Shakespeare, Performance, Self*.
    London and New York: Routledge, 2005.
Etchells, Tim. *Certain Fragments: Forced Entertainment and Contemporary
    Performance*. London and New York: Routledge, 1999.
Fusco, Coco. *The Bodies That Were Not Ours and Other Writings*. London
    and New York: Routledge, 2001.

Hallward, Peter. 'Staging Equality: On Rancière's Theatocracy.' *New Left Review* 37 (2006): 109–29.

Handke, Peter. 'Street-Theater and Theater-Theater.' Trans. Joel Agee. *Essays on German Theater*. Ed. Margaret Herzfeld-Sander. New York: Continuum, 1985. 311–15.

Harding, James M., and John Rouse. *Not the Other Avant-Garde: The Transnational Foundations of Avant-Garde Performance*. Ann Arbor: U of Michigan P, 2006.

Harvie, Jen. *Staging the UK*. Manchester and New York: Manchester UP, 2005.

Heritage, Paul. 'The Promise of Performance: True Love/Real Love.' *Theatre Matters: Performance and Culture on the World Stage*. Eds. Richard Boon and Jane Plastow. Cambridge: Cambridge UP, 1998. 154–75.

Jameson, Fredric. *Brecht and Method*. London and New York: Verso, 2000.

Kelleher, Joe, and Nicholas Ridout, eds. *Contemporary Theatres in Europe: A Critical Companion*. London and New York: Routledge, 2007.

Kershaw, Baz. *The Politics of Performance: Radical Theatre As Cultural Intervention*. London and New York: Routledge, 1992.

————. *The Radical in Performance: Between Brecht and Baudrillard*. London and New York: Routledge, 1999.

Kruger, Loren. *Post-Imperial Brecht: Politics and Performance, East and South*. Cambridge: Cambridge UP, 2004.

Kunst, Bojana. 'Politics of Affection and Uneasiness.' *Maska* 5–6 (2003): 23–6.

Lehmann, Hans-Thies. *Postdramatic Theatre*. Trans. Karen Jürs-Munby. London and New York: Routledge, 2006.

Levi, Primo. *The Search for Roots: A Personal Anthology*. Trans. Peter Forbes. London: Allen Lane, 2001.

Martin, Bradford D. *The Theater Is in the Street: Politics and Performance in Sixties America*. Amherst and Boston: U of Massachusetts P, 2004.

Pearson, Michael, and Michael Shanks. *Theatre/Archaeology*. London and New York: Routledge, 2001.

Phelan, Peggy. *Unmarked: The Politics of Performance*. London and New York: Routledge, 1993.

Plato. *Gorgias*. Trans. W. Hamilton. Harmondsworth, UK: Penguin, 1987.

————. *The Laws*. Trans. T. J. Saunders. London: Penguin, 2004.

————. *The Republic*. Trans. D. Lee. London: Penguin, 2007.

Rancière, Jacques. 'Ten Theses on Politics.' *Theory & Event* 5.3 (2001). 28 December 2008 <http://muse.jhu.edu/journals/theory_and_event/>.

————. 'Introducing Disagreement.' *Angelaki* 9.1 (2004): 3–9.

————. 'The Emancipated Spectator.' *Artforum* March 2007: 271–80.

Read, Alan. *Theatre, Intimacy & Engagement: The Last Human Venue*. London: Palgrave Macmillan, 2007.

Ridout, Nicholas. *Stage Fright, Animals, and Other Theatrical Problems*. Cambridge: Cambridge UP, 2006.

Rokem, Freddie. *Performing History: Theatrical Representations of the Past in Contemporary Theatre*. Iowa City: U of Iowa P, 2007.

Samuel, Raphael, Ewan MacColl, and Stuart Cosgrove. *Theatres of the Left 1880–1935: Workers' Theatre Movements in Britain and America*. London: Routledge & Kegan Paul, 1985.

Schneider, Rebecca. *The Explicit Body in Performance*. London and New York: Routledge, 1997.

Szondi, Peter. *Theory of the Modern Drama*. Minneapolis: U of Minnesota P, 1987.

Taylor, Diana. *The Repertoire and the Archive: Performing Cultural Memory in the Americas*. Durham, NC: Duke UP, 2003.

tucker green, debbie. *Random*. London: Royal Court/Nick Hern Books, 2008.

Vasconcelos, Luiz. 'Eyewitness 11.03.08.' Photograph. *Guardian* 13 March 2008.

Weber, Samuel. *Theatricality As Medium*. New York: Fordham UP, 2004.

Williams, Raymond. *Drama from Ibsen to Brecht*. London: Pelican, 1973.

————. *Writing in Society*. London and New York: Verso, 1983.

index

83

acknowledgements

Extracts from debbie tucker green's *random* (copyright © 2008 debbie tucker green) are quoted with permission from Nick Hern Books Limited, London (http://www.nickhernbooks. co.uk).

I would like to thank Dan Rebellato, a most diligent editor, and Aoife Monks, the most perceptive of readers, both of whom saw through to how it could be better. I remain indebted.

Introducing **Theatre&**, a **vibrant** and **eye-catching** new series of **'short, sharp shots'** for theatre students

978-0-230-21028-8

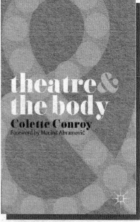

978-0-230-20543-7

small books on theatre & everything else

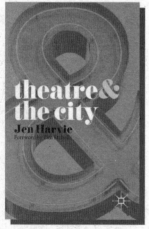

978-0-230-20522-2

978-0-230-21857-4

Presenting the **BEST WRITING** from **'A-list'** scholars